The American Novel series provides students of American literature with introductory critical guides to great works of American literature. Each volume begins with a substantial introduction by a distinguished authority on the text, giving details of the work's composition, publication history, and contemporary reception, as well as a survey of the major critical trends and readings from first publication to the present. This overview is followed by a group of new essays, each specially commissioned from a leading scholar in the field, which together constitute a forum of interpretative methods and prominent contemporary ideas on the text. There are also helpful guides to further reading. Specifically designed for undergraduates, the series will be a powerful resource for anyone engaged in the critical analysis of major American novels and other important texts.

Go Down, Moses (1942) came to fruition during the Second World War, was written during one of Faulkner's most traumatic periods, and has fallen into critical neglect amid the vast scholarship on the great southern writer. In part, this collection aims to tilt the balance, forcing the reader beyond critical commonplaces through asking challenging questions. The five essays assembled here explore the tensions of race and gender apparent throughout the novel. Judith Sensibar approaches the work through Faulkner's relationship with Caroline Barr, the black woman who was his primary caretaker in life; Judith Wittenberg offers an ecological reading, setting the work firmly within its chronological age; John T. Matthews redefines the novel as a "southern" experience; Minrose Gwin focuses on the spaces in the text occupied by black women characters; and Thadious M. Davis charts further complications of the black–white relationships that lie at the heart of the novel.

NEW ESSAYS ON GO DOWN, MOSES

★ THE AMERICAN NOVEL ★

GENERAL EDITOR

Emory Elliott
University of California, Riverside

Other works in the series:

New Essays on
Go Down, Moses

Edited by
Linda Wagner-Martin

Published by the Press Syndicate of the University of Cambridge
The Pitt Building, Trumpington Street, Cambridge CB2 1RP
40 West 20th Street, New York, NY 10011-4211, USA
10 Stamford Road, Oakleigh, Melbourne 3166, Australia

First published 1996

Printed in the United States of America

Library of Congress Cataloging-in-Publication Data
New essays on Go down, Moses / edited by Linda Wagner-Martin.
        p.   cm. – (The American novel)
Includes bibliographical references (p.   ).
ISBN 0-521-45431-X (hardback). – ISBN 0-521-45609-6 (paperback)
  1. Faulkner, William, 1897–1962. Go down, Moses. 2. Afro-
American women in literature.   3. Southern States – In literature.
  4. Race relations in literature.   I. Wagner-Martin, Linda.
                II. Series.
            PS3511.A86G6375   1996
            813'.52 – dc20   95-9466

A catalog record for this book is available from the British Library.

ISBN 0-521-45431-X hardback
ISBN 0-521-45609-6 paperback

Contents

v

Contents

Series Editor's Preface

In literary criticism the last twenty-five years have been particularly fruitful. Since the rise of the New Criticism in the 1950s, which focused attention of critics and readers upon the text itself – apart from history, biography, and society – there has emerged a wide variety of critical methods which have brought to literary works a rich diversity of perspectives: social, historical, political, psychological, economic, ideological, and philosophical. While attention to the text itself, as taught by the New Critics, remains at the core of contemporary interpretation, the widely shared assumption that works of art generate many different kinds of interpretations has opened up possibilities for new readings and new meanings.

Before this critical revolution, many works of American literature had come to be taken for granted by earlier generations of readers as having an established set of recognized interpretations. There was a sense among many students that the canon was established and that the larger thematic and interpretative issues had been decided. The task of the new reader was to examine the ways in which elements such as structure, style, and imagery contributed to each novel's acknowledged purpose. But recent criticism has brought these old assumptions into question and has thereby generated a wide variety of original, and often quite surprising, interpretations of the classics, as well as of rediscovered works such as Kate Chopin's *The Awakening,* which has only recently entered the canon of works that scholars and critics study and that teachers assign their students.

The aim of The American Novel Series is to provide students of American literature and culture with introductory critical guides to American novels and other important texts now widely read and studied. Usually devoted to a single work, each volume begins with an introduction by the volume editor, a distinguished authority on the text. The introduction presents details of the work's composition, publication history, and contemporary reception, as well as a survey of the major critical trends and readings from first publication to the present. This overview is followed by four or five original essays, specifically commissioned from senior scholars of established reputation and from outstanding younger critics. Each essay presents a distinct point of view, and together they constitute a forum of interpretative methods and of the best contemporary ideas on each text.

It is our hope that these volumes will convey the vitality of current critical work in American literature, generate new insights and excitement for students of American literature, and inspire new respect for and new perspectives upon these major literary texts.

Emory Elliott
University of California, Riverside

1

Introduction

LINDA WAGNER-MARTIN

G*O Down, Moses* was published May 11, 1942. Over a year
before, in January of 1941, William Faulkner – the author
of more than a dozen novels and story collections – had written
Harold Ober, his agent, "Thank you for the money. I did not
intend the wire to ask for a loan, but I have used the money and
I thank you for it.... When I wired you I did not have $15.00
to pay electricity bill with, keep my lights burning."[1] Scarcely
eight years after that letter, Faulkner was honored with the most
prestigious literary award in the world – the 1949 Nobel Prize for
Literature and with it, a check for more than thirty thousand
dollars.[2] (He had also been elected to membership in both the
National Institute of Arts and Letters and the American Academy
of Arts and Letters. From the latter, in 1950, he received the
Howells Medal for Fiction, and for his *Collected Stories* in 1951 he
received the National Book Award.)[3] The juxtaposition of these
events suggests the vicissitudes that marked Faulkner's career as
America's foremost twentieth-century novelist. During the middle period of Faulkner's life, nothing was secure – not literary
reputation, or finances, or marriage, or family standing. Yet from
the agonized, and agonizing, decade of the author's forties came
one of his greatest works – *Go Down, Moses*.

The novel may have originated from Faulkner's desperate
financial straits. Trying to support his wife and child, and Estelle's
two children from her first marriage, Faulkner also considered
himself responsible for his dead brother's family (Dean had been
killed while flying in 1935), and for his mother's well-being.[4] He
had learned to earn money from writing and marketing short
stories (which paid better individually than did many of his

novels) and had written film scripts in Hollywood for part of each year from 1932 through 1937. In 1938, comparatively prosperous from the sale of film rights to *The Unvanquished,* he had purchased Greenfield Farm. That property, combined with Rowan Oak, the house and grounds he had bought in 1932, added to his already heavy financial burden. His economic worries contributed to his personal instability, evident in his recurring – and increasing – bouts with alcoholism.

Rather than return to Hollywood, which he disliked, Faulkner tried to publish a novel each year: after 1936, when *Absalom, Absalom!* appeared, in early 1938 he brought out *The Unvanquished;* 1939 saw *The Wild Palms;* 1940, *The Hamlet.* The last three works were comprised, at least partly, of his previously published short stories; *The Unvanquished* was a collage of narratives, retitled and organized to shape a novel. It was not surprising, then, that in 1940 Faulkner asked his editor Robert Haas about the possibility of Random House's giving him a large advance on a novel manuscript built around what he called "the negro stories."[5] He needed a book for the 1941 season.

After much discussion, with Faulkner even considering a move to another publishing house, Haas came through with a thousand dollar advance (which Faulkner divided among his creditors), and Faulkner eventually sent in the much revised manuscript for his new novel. Imagine his surprise, then, when he opened the mailing packet months later, to see on the novel's cover the words, *Go Down, Moses and Other Stories.*[6]

* * * * *

Given the title, reviewers had little choice other than to assume the work was a story collection,[7] and much of its reputation even into the present has been as a group of seven stories. Of the group, "The Bear" has received an immense amount of attention, as it did from the start. Milton Rugoff, reviewing the book for the influential *New York Herald-Tribune,* compared "The Bear" to Herman Melville's *Moby-Dick,* saying that each illustrated "the mysterious teleology of nature."[8] Emphasizing the importance of the primordial, of man's relationship to nature, led to the tendency to see Ike McCaslin (the young Isaac of "The Bear" and "The Old People") as the novel's central consciousness. As Lionel Trilling put it, Ike seems heroic because he values the "dignity of freedom" in the midst of more grasping McCaslins.[9] For another reviewer, the Ike McCaslin story was a bildungsroman, following the growth of the young man into adulthood – a familiar, and usually optimistic, narrative.[10]

In early reviews, however, "The Bear" received somewhat less attention than did the disjuncture between "Pantaloon in Black" and the Lucas (McCaslin) Beauchamp stories (the title story and the novella, "The Fire and the Hearth"). A common complaint was that Rider (from "Pantaloon") seemed not to *be* a "McCaslin": therefore, how was the reader to relate that story to the rest of the book? Although the *Times Literary Supplement* found "Pantaloon in Black" the most impressive section of the book, Trilling thought it inferior.

So far as the book's overall structure was concerned, many reviewers accepted its unity – whether they considered it novel or collection. Ironically, one of the harshest judges of its format was Malcolm Cowley, the critic who would soon edit *The Portable Faulkner* anthology for Viking Press, a collection that did much to bring Faulkner's writing to the attention of serious American readers. In his 1942 review, however, Cowley described *Go Down, Moses* as a "loosely jointed" collection, which only masqueraded as a novel. In reality, Cowley said, most of the stories had either been published in magazines, or had at least been written for that market.[11]

Several negative reviewers pointedly described *Go Down, Moses* as a characteristic Faulkner text, filled as it was with "miscegenation, rot, murder, and ruin."[12] John Temple Graves denied any tone of humor to the varied narratives and Philip Toynbee said the novel was symptomatic of Faulkner's artistic exhaustion.[13] Alfred Kazin's assessment was that Faulkner was a bitter man because he had been made an outsider in the contemporary South. No longer part of a social elite, he voiced his displeasure with the world through characters so abstract they had little identity. Faulkner's difficult style, Kazin said, was an attempt to disguise the emptiness at the heart of both his work and his vision.[14]

In his 1942 study, *Writers in Crisis*, Maxwell Geismar vented his objection to what he saw as Faulkner's success. For Geismar, Faulkner's coupling of violence with incest, rape, and miscegenation proved his personal misogyny. Calling the author a "fascist," a word which in 1942 had even stronger negative connotations than it does today, Geismar said that Faulkner laid the fall of the South to the emancipation of both blacks and women.[15] It was Faulkner's use of black characters that seemed to baffle some critics. Samuel Putnam said that Faulkner's portrayal of "the Negro" signaled "horror and human defeat," with the black "portrayed as a hopelessly forlorn and trapped creature." Putnam concludes that "Faulkner has not progressed as Erskine Caldwell has."[16] That the anonymous *TLS* reviewer was convinced, in contrast, that Faulkner held a deep "fraternal sentiment" for the "Mississippi Negro as he was and is"[17] suggests that Geismar's and Putnam's readings were at the edge of a continuum of interpretations. The disparity among such readings reflects a common problem, the sheer difficulty of reading the modernist text.

Unlikely as it was that readers would find only the horrific in *Go Down, Moses*, the by then pervasive attitudes about Faulkner's sometimes shocking and violent work influenced some of these 1942 comments. Coming to the novelist's defense were both Warren Beck and Cleanth Brooks, whose later studies would do much to build a sympathetic and informed readership for Faulkner. Beck – calling the author the most brilliant of American novelists – stated that whenever critics complained about Faulkner's style, they were admitting their own failures as good readers. Brooks defended not only Faulkner's way of expressing his ideas but the ideas themselves, claiming that his philosophy was often misread. Faulkner is a "tragedian," Brooks said, free from the cynicism and sensationalism he was sometimes charged with.[18]

* * * * *

At least partly because of the error in the original titling of the novel, criticism of *Go Down, Moses* has been slow to cohere. Much criticism of the 1960s and 1970s, and even the 1980s, still discussed the book's genre. More substantive critical problems remained beneath the surface, although attention to other of Faulkner's novels had become varied and sophisticated. Several of the more troubling critical issues arose when critics tried to fit *Go Down, Moses* into Faulkner's oeuvre.

By the late 1930s, Faulkner critics had begun to understand how great a writer the young Mississippian really was. The creator of not only the potboilers that had brought him a kind of fame – i.e., *Sanctuary* – Faulkner deserved to be read as the American Joyce or Proust (both of whom were writers he knew well). In defending Faulkner's intricately modernist work, such critics as Conrad Aiken, George Marion O'Donnell, and Delmore Schwartz[19] discussed his early novels – *The Sound and the Fury, As I Lay Dying, Light in August*. A body of substantial criticism on these works was thus early in place. When *Absalom, Absalom!* was published in 1936, with Quentin Compson, the most sympathetic character from *The Sound and the Fury* resurrected, as it were, after his suicide in the 1929 novel, critical attention to the linked books intensified. The two novels provided – and still provide – a focal point for discussion meant to illuminate all of Faulkner's writing.

For several reasons, such a focus will not work. As Michael Millgate pointed out decades ago, Faulkner's genius led him to write widely varied fictions.[20] Particularly in his later work, change occurred not only in his choices of narrative design and points of view, but also and even more dramatically in his subject matter. To ignore what are often crucial changes places the reader at risk. Put simply, Isaac McCaslin, often read as the protagonist of *Go Down, Moses,* is not another Quentin Compson. By 1942, Faulkner had stopped romanticizing his inheritance of southern history, tradition, legend, and myth. *Go Down, Moses* is, in many aspects, a representation of the way the South must relinquish its arcane values. Rather than despairing over the region's losses, as Quentin Compson and his father did, healthy Southerners have more apt choices. One of Ike McCaslin's roles in *Go Down, Moses* is to represent the notion of choice. As he comes to see the corruption inherent in the McCaslin lineage, Ike chooses to disown his birthright. But as Faulkner shows in *Go Down, Moses,* the mess of pottage he accepts in exchange for property – living on with the crude descendants of his peers, "uncle to half a county and father to no one"[21] – comes under scrutiny, too. Faulkner's representation of the once idyllic hunting camp shows its participants, and their activities, to be as flawed as Lucius Quintus Carothers McCaslin was, at least in his rape of his black slave Eunice and, later, of their daughter Tomasina (Tomy). McCaslin's sexual depravity led both women – directly – to their early deaths.

The irresponsible father, like the absent mother, is a staple character in Faulkner's novels. But unlike Bundren in *As I Lay Dying,* or both Sutpen and Coldfield in *Absalom, Absalom!,*[22] the McCaslin story in *Go Down, Moses* gives the plot new intensity. In Faulkner's earlier novels, the narratives delighted in extending the impasse of a conundrum past the book's ending – so that the reader's strategy, in part, is to accept the impossibility of "knowing." In *Go Down, Moses,* however, Faulkner forces the reader to know. Awareness penetrates the reader as it has Ike McCaslin.

Instead of forcing the reader to a willed passivity, however, as it did Ike, Faulkner's narrative suggests other courses of action. The reader is made to realize that the horrors of the abusive family romance plot must be faced: Someone must assume responsibility. Ike at least faces the incest in his lineage. But it is likely that Faulkner intends the reader to see that McCaslin's reaction – his renunciation of his patrimony and of his role in both family and community – does not help anyone.[23] His absconding, in fact, allows Roth Edmonds to live the unexamined life of his forebears, with no alternative community voice to check or reprove him.

Faulkner's focus on Edmonds' self-gratifying affair with the unnamed mulatto, who is one of his own cousins within the McCaslin line, provides each reader a Rorschach inkblot test. Edmonds' choice of abandoning his lover and their son in order to stay within the white male community (idealized in the hunting camp), complete with that community's obvious and ribald devaluation/commodification of women, identifies one crumbling moral strand within the traditional patriarchal system.

Go Down, Moses is, then, the beginning of Faulkner's mature statement about responsibility. Difficult as its structure is, forcing the reader literally to put together glimpses of information – often as indecipherable as the cryptic writing in the commissary books – Faulkner's novel replicates the process of a mind coming to understanding. It is as if Faulkner himself needed, in writing the book,[24] to be led to the meaning of his own fictional statement. Six years previous, Quentin's narrative in *Absalom, Absalom!* marked a definite end to Faulkner's use of narrative form to interrogate, expand, and finally confound whatever ostensible "story" he is telling. What really happens in *Absalom, Absalom!* is blockage. Quentin cannot face the truth about either the South or himself, as his dramatically highlighted closing words show. Mr. Compson, blind to the implications of sterility in his recounting of the Sutpen tale and caught in fantasy as he shapes that story on the hook of Rosa Coldfield's frustrated life and death, gives in to endless repetition, to a circling interrogation of "facts" that are not in question, and to blatant falsification whenever he wants to deny Rosa's more literal tale.

Michael Millgate has seen *Go Down, Moses* as the culmination of Faulkner's greatest period of creation;[25] I would propose that this 1942 novel is, in some ways, a new start. In it, Faulkner begins to attempt expressing what it feels like to be the heir of white patriarchal power in a slave state, what it feels like to be the wellborn son, the wellborn *white* son, of a family hardly memorable for its stability or sanity. Ironically, what the Falkners – like the Sartorises of Faulkner's Yoknapatawpha County – were known for was foolhardiness. Rash intemperance of both spirit and personality was their trademark; and the young writer, nicknamed "Count No 'Count" as he wore his RAF uniform during the postwar years in Oxford, had heretofore prided himself on being the great-grandson who carried on The Colonel's fascinating exploits (as well as both his fiction and his irascible moodiness).

After forty years of privileging irresponsibility in his own life, romanticizing its foibles, glorifying its legends – both in oral story telling and in writing – William Faulkner fell through to the truth: that all the romance in the world, all the glories of fame, all the alluring tropes of recognition, could not substitute for living a humane life that valued other people, black as well as white. *Go Down, Moses* was his testament of adulthood. In that novel, he challenged the definition of "normal" about a number of classically male behaviors: drinking, manipulating friends and family, showing little feeling, sacrificing love for wealth, hiding from responsibility through traditional male bonding activities such as hunting, playing poker, chasing women, bragging about sexual conquests. It was a definite reversal in theme. It was such a reversal, narratively, that even Faulkner's most alert readers found making sense of *Go Down, Moses* difficult. They had for years been reading Faulkner's brilliantly experimental texts. *Go Down, Moses* was no more difficult than many other of his works. What made readers struggle with the work, with conceptualizing *Go Down, Moses* as a whole, was that Faulkner seemed finally to be making pronouncements substantially different from those of *Absalom, Absalom!*

In that novel, as in most of his other earlier works, the author had valued immersion in the past. To ferret out that past seemed one reason Faulkner resurrected the character of Quentin Compson, to re-explore the decline of the modern southern family, the values of the traditional patriarchy in conflict with the new materialism that devalued family ties, tradition, and history. *Absalom, Absalom!* sets Quentin's quest in a wider context, suggesting that those values are suspect, if not self-serving. In southern history, Sutpen's Hundred serves no viable purpose, either social or familial.[26] Thomas Sutpen is shown to be little but animal, mating where and when he can, caring nothing for either his sex partners or their offspring. His abuse of Ellen parallels the contempt he evinced for Charles Bon's mother, for Rosa, and for Millie, whose "correctly" sexed – i.e., male – child would have earned for her at best a stable in the barn.

The romantic concept of "heroic" male, of man strong enough and disciplined enough to take possession of untamed earth, describes the creator of "Sutpen's Hundred." But within *Absalom,*

Absalom! Faulkner clearly showed Sutpen's strength to be misguided and misspent. An insulated, maniacally obsessive man, Sutpen used his superhuman physical and intellectual powers for nothing.

* * * * *

Although it may appear that Ike's life, too, has led to "nothing," at least in a material evaluation, Faulkner had written important definitional books between 1936, when *Absalom, Absalom!* was published, and the completion of *Go Down, Moses* in 1941. In *The Wild Palms*, for example, he worked through concepts of "love"; in *The Unvanquished*, concepts of "honor"; and in both – and also in *Pylon*, where such discussion is the basis for the parodic musings of the Reporter – concepts of "power," especially the power of patriarchy. His 1940 *The Hamlet* was a foray into the ways in which parody might enable readers to see more accurate meanings for all those abstract concepts. But comedy failed him, at least insofar as readers apprehending his intentions, so in *Go Down, Moses* he returned to the somber tone that had increasingly marked his writing in the 1930s.

To indicate the seriousness of his undertaking, Faulkner chose as title for both the novel and one of its most poignant episodes the title and refrain of the spiritual, "Go Down, Moses." With the injunction from God that the Egyptians "Let my people go," Moses led the Israelites out of bondage – and so too would black slaves be led to freedom. ("Go Down, Moses," first printed in 1861, was a key abolitionist spiritual.)

> Go down, Moses,
> 'Way down in Egypt's land.
> Tell ole Pharaoh,
> Let my people go.

The integrity of a captive people – subject to inhuman treatment but still believing in salvation – is the keystone image for this novel. When critics have suggested that "The McCaslins" would have been a more directive title,[27] they overlook the resonance of both the painful – because realistic – expectation and promise which "Go Down, Moses" as title provides. It suggests Faulkner's undertaking: to write a shameful, and shaming, story, rather than a prideful one.

In writing this novel Faulkner reconceptualized the role of memory. As Nicole Moulineux points out in a comparison of Faulkner and Proust, Faulkner's memories are seldom "soothing and restorative" but instead "torturing and destructive" (at least to such characters as Quentin). Faulkner's narratives depict "the memory of suffering, humiliation, and defeat. More often than not, remembering is a way of grieving. It may bring knowledge, perhaps even a bitter wisdom; it never brings true comfort."[28] In a Nietzschean reading, Richard King contends that Faulkner's questioning of the values of his traditional, patriarchal culture is tantamount to erasing memory. Once the reader questions cultural values and begins "to suspect that the claims of the past are deadening, life-threatening claims," King asks, "How can we remember and represent what is dismembered and absent?" For this critic, Ike McCaslin's withdrawal illustrates the tragedy of being caught "between . . . at the closing time of one's culture and prior to the time when a new order of binding authority has emerged." But as King admits, Ike's shame differs from Quentin's in that it is anything but abstract: The degradation he sees exists in *his* family, a unit still dominated by the commissary ledgers and their repeated phrase, "Fathers will."[29]

Criticism of the past fifteen years has begun to read *Go Down, Moses* as something other than a collection of stories, a continuation of *Absalom, Absalom!*, or a work of secondary importance. Books devoted to exploring the writing of *Go Down, Moses* appeared during the 1970s and early 1980s – James Early's *The Making of Go Down, Moses*[30] in 1972; Joanne V. Creighton's *William Faulkner's Craft of Revision* in 1977; and *Threads Cable Strong: William Faulkner's Go Down, Moses* by Dirk Kuyk, Jr., in 1983. Such studies affirmed the importance of the work.

The greater shift in criticism of *Go Down, Moses*, however, was in the view of Faulkner's melding white narratives with black. No longer seen as charming or sentimental, primitive or embarrassing, the racially bifurcated story of the McCaslin lineage was understood to be the book's center. In the words of Philip Weinstein, who praises criticism of the 1980s such as that by Thadious Davis, Erskine Peters, John Matthews, James Snead, Eric Sundquist, and others, "race relations and distinctions shifted in Faulkner's own career from the status of topic to obsession." The writer's later works, accordingly, show "an increasingly powerful grasp of racism as a *discursive* dynamic: a disease perpetuated through language practices. That immersion seems to have produced in him as well a painful recognition of the alterable yet ineradicable role of racist tropes within his own 'unique' discourse."[31]

Characteristic of more recent readings, the work of some critics has persuaded readers that racism is inherent in patriarchy. Wesley Morris suggests, "Racism is a version of paternalism. . . . sins of racial violence are supplementations of the primal sin against the father, the violation of the prohibition of sexual union with the (m)other."[32] In Mick Gidley's view, Faulkner works regularly with "plots of patrimony."[33] Such a reading dovetails with James Snead's privileging of *Go Down, Moses* because "overriding metaphors of the bear-hunt, the slave-hunt, and the treasure-hunt all signify potential failures for the dominant hunter because he no longer sets the rules. Hunting, as a reciprocal act, often unpleasurably upends accustomed hierarchies of subject and object."[34]

More explicit commentary returns to simpler thematic proofs. Like Daniel Hoffman, Albert J. Devlin points out that Faulkner's black characters "share intimate relationships that affirm their engagement with life itself," citing Rider's "deep, transforming love for Mannie" as well as the passions of Lucas and Turl and Roth's mistress.[35] Leon Forrest grounds Faulkner's effectiveness as writer during this period in his "respect for the significance of black folklore; his willingness to explore some of the ranges of racism . . . ; his willingness to confront the racial agony of the South, and to eloquently lift this travail to stage center, as the ever constant moral issue at the very heart and soul of this Republic." Forrest goes further to claim that Faulkner's involvement in racial themes serves as catalyst for his best writing: "the powerful presence of the black agony, in his vaulting imagination, provided Faulkner with the essential materiality for his greatest novels and the towering and tragic vision."[36]

Not all critics have praised Faulkner's treatment of black culture and characters. Myra Jehlen, calling his presentation of the South an example of "voluntary segregation," finds little authenticity in any of *Go Down, Moses* except "Pantaloon in Black." Because she resents Faulkner giving his readers such stereotypes of black personalities, she finds his equally stereotypical dedication of the book to his "mammy," Caroline Barr, ironically appropriate. Diane Roberts' 1994 book, *Faulkner and Southern Womanhood*, counters Jehlen's objections, claiming that Faulkner's black characters are not drawn from stereotypes. Placing the author in historical context, Roberts argues, "Faulkner wrote out of particular moments in history. . . . He had to accommodate contradictory meanings for blackness and could, of course, achieve only incompleteness, pulled between a progressive sympathy for blacks and a nostalgia for the days of stable categories of black and white."[37]

Judith Lockyer's objections are that Faulkner uses the character of Gavin Stevens to provide a realistic portrayal of white reaction to black grief – she claims that Faulkner shares Stevens' discomfort (in the "Go Down, Moses" chapter, shut out of mourning with Mollie and her friends) – because he cannot approach either the language, or the emotions, of his black characters. "Faulkner reaches the limits of his own capacity to understand and to imagine the black consciousness, and thus to write the black voice. . . . Faulkner's black characters, as well as his women, show us the limitations of a language that acknowledges the presence of the other. Because the female and black characters are radically different from their author, they allow us to see them more clearly as projections of a single consciousness."[38]

From Carolyn Porter's very recent perspective, using Lacanian models might argue against a simple condemnation of Faulkner's attempts. As Porter explains, "In the Imaginary register – where life is mostly lived, as Lacanian theory has it – 'woman' may represent absence, separation and loss, and so forth, but viewed from the vantage point provided by the Symbolic, women are still subjects, speaking subjects, no matter how occulted their position." Within Faulkner's texts, woman is recognized as Other, but she does appear, and she does have access to voice. Porter parallels Faulkner's treatment of women (white and black) with that of black (usually male) characters, pointing to the figure of Lucas Beauchamp as representative of the survival of a patriarchy built on slave labor and dependent on the black slave woman for its reproduction of that labor.[39] Essays by both Judith Sensibar and Minrose Gwin included in this collection contribute to, and usefully augment, these discussions.

The issue for Philip Weinstein is not that Faulkner's abilities in drawing black characters and white women characters are similarly limited, but that the author avoids working with portrayals of women at all. Weinstein describes *Go Down, Moses* as an atypical text because in it Faulkner "focuses with unprecedented intensity upon black males. . . . the black women here have no such instigating power. Rousing desire in others but narratively deprived of it themselves, they rarely escape the tragic, but passive, role of being taken and abandoned by their white lovers."[40]

Although Elisabeth Muhlenfeld agrees that Faulkner presents very few women in this novel, as if attempting to create some Edenic "man's world," she contends that "the women in *Go Down, Moses* carry great artistic weight." Contrasted at every narrative turn with Faulkner's largely passive male characters, each of these women – black as well as white – "is a taker of risks, willing to sacrifice things as precious as reputation, wealth, life itself, to preserve the integrity of the family and the value of life itself." Speaking directly of Eunice's suicide, Muhlenfeld argues that her death reflects her powerlessness to protect either herself or her daughter while she lives; her death, however, "not only shames the race who so wronged and dehumanized her but also empowers her descendants."[41]

Fascinated as the critical world is now with issues of race and gender which are both new and significant, there are still other ways of approaching Faulkner's *Go Down, Moses*. For Michael Grimwood, the novel is the sign of the writer's personal exhaustion: "The central subject of 'Delta Autumn' is not race relations or the failure of love, or the wilderness, but the gradual depletion of energy from the earth, from history, from men's lives, from Faulkner's career." In calling *Go Down, Moses* an account of "the ultimate depletion,"[42] Grimwood reverses the usual stance in reading Faulkner, the stance which avoids autobiography. Rarely do critics explore Faulkner's fiction by using biographical or psychoanalytic methods, but Eric Sundquist, too, terms this book "Faulkner's most honest and personally revealing novel." Sundquist directs his statement toward what Faulkner as author

does not or can no longer say. *Go Down, Moses* illustrates this in two powerful and telling instances – in Ike McCaslin and Lucas Beauchamp, the two characters on whom Faulkner seems to spend his best powers as they dwindle into two different, but intimately related, failed visions. Ike's relinquishing of his patrimony resembles, in authorial terms, Faulkner's own, for never again does his power to imagine the burden of that inheritance . . . reappear with such expressive dignity. And never again does Faulkner . . . approach the tragic dignity of a "black" character he momentarily discovered in Lucas Beauchamp.[43]

Echoing Leon Forrest's contention that Faulkner's involvement in the crucible of racial issues called forth the best of his imaginative power, Sundquist implies a duality of character both white and black – that both Ike and Lucas are prototypes of the middle-aging Faulkner.

For Karl Zender, the analogous character is the negatively drawn Roth Edmonds, like Faulkner in his early forties, and like Faulkner "a man driven almost to distraction by the demands, both social and economic, being made on him." Hasty and irascible, capable of good judgments but with no time to make them, Edmonds is the patriarch of a farm that resembles Faulkner's Greenfield Farm; and his relationship with Lucas Beauchamp parallels Faulkner's tenuous relations with Ned Barnett, "a long-time family servant" who was in some ways as integral to the writer's life as Caroline Barr had been.[44]

Zender's emphasis on Faulkner's financial plight – and the embarrassment it often caused him – has validity. As we have seen, borrowing the money to pay his light bill troubled William Faulkner inordinately; and to place characters out of the daily realm of practical action (as he does Isaac McCaslin, and in some

14

ways Lucas Beauchamp) is to suggest somewhat wistfully the luxury of such withdrawal. In Professor Davis's assessment of the economic codes of the times and the legal ramifications of definitions of ownership, a different set of issues impacts on the reading of the novel, particularly of the role of Tomey's Turl.

The editor of this collection hopes that these five important new essays show the centrality of this novel to both Faulkner's continually developing thematic patterns and the real world of his readers then and now. Rather than being considered one of his most difficult works, *Go Down, Moses* deserves to be championed as a necessarily intricate composite text, strident voice set against controlled, passive withdrawal set against raging mourning, apparent comedy undercut repeatedly by an authorial attention to silences as poignant as dialogue.

This collection aims also to bring criticism of *Go Down, Moses* into alignment with that of Faulkner's other major works. The hard interrogation of each of these stunning essays forces the reader to do more than repeat critical commonplaces – however comfortable – from the past. Essays by Judith Sensibar and Minrose Gwin discuss, among other points, the vexed issue of why Faulkner draws his women characters – particularly his black women characters – as he does. Those by Professors Wittenberg and Matthews place *Go Down, Moses* in a somewhat wider cultural context. Professor Wittenberg's speculation that Faulkner turned later in his career to matters of ecological interest (as in the prose sections of *Requiem for a Nun* and *The Big Woods*, as well as in this novel) anticipates Professor Matthews' concern with new ways of envisioning Faulkner as part of a South viewed both sociologically and economically. His rich study of Faulkner as a southern writer in this wide definition provides a perspective useful to the reading of many of Faulkner's novels.

NOTES

1 William Faulkner to Harold Ober, January 18, 1941, in *Selected Letters of William Faulkner*, ed. Joseph Blotner. New York: Random House, 1977, pp. 138–139. (Future references will be to SLWF.)

2 Joseph Blotner, *Faulkner, A Biography.* New York: Random House, 1984, p. 523.

3 Ibid., p. 750.

4 As Faulkner wrote in May, 1940,

> Beginning at the age of thirty I, an artist, a sincere one and of the first class, who should be free even of his own economic responsibilities . . . began to become the sole, principal and partial support – food, shelter, heat, clothes, medicine, kotex, school fees, toilet paper and picture shows – of my mother, . . . brother and his wife and two sons, another brother's widow and child, a wife of my own, and two step children, my own child; I inherited my father's debts and his dependents, white and black. (Quoted in Blotner, *Faulkner,* p. 417)

5 Blotner, *Faulkner,* p. 420.

6 Faulkner wrote later about "the shock (mild) I got when I saw the printed title page" (in SLWF, 284).

7 For example, Horace Gregory, "New Tales by William Faulkner," *New York Times Book Review* (May 10, 1942), p. 4; William Abrahams, "William Faulkner at His Best in Collection of Seven Stories," Boston *Daily Globe* (May 6, 1942), p. 19F; C. B. Boutell, "Series of Seven Faulkner Tales," Boston *Herald* (May 13, 1942), p. 17M; and, among others, Jack Keller, "Faulkner's Southern Stories Gather Under One Title," Columbus *Citizen* (May 24, 1942), Magazine, p. 4.

8 Milton Rugoff, "The Magic of William Faulkner," *New York Herald-Tribune Books* (May 17, 1942), p. 1. See Eric J. Sundquist for a discussion of the comparison (*Faulkner: The House Divided* [Baltimore: Johns Hopkins University Press, 1983]).

9 Lionel Trilling, "The McCaslins of Mississippi," *The Nation* (May 30, 1942), pp. 632–633.

10 Anonymous, "Faulkneresque," *Times Literary Supplement* (October 10, 1942), p. 497.

11 Malcolm Cowley, "Go Down to Faulkner's Land," *The New Republic* (June 29, 1942), p. 900.

12 John Temple Graves, "Faulkner. . . ," *Saturday Review,* 25 (May 2, 1942), p. 16.

13 Philip Toynbee, "Review of *Go Down, Moses,*" *New Statesman and Nation,* 24 (October 31, 1942), p. 293.

14 Alfred Kazin, "Faulkner: The Rhetoric and the Agony," *Virginia Quarterly Review,* 18 (Summer 1942), pp. 390–391.

15 Maxwell Geismar, *Writers in Crisis* (Boston: Houghton Mifflin, 1942), p. 179.

16 Samuel Putnam, "Quaint, Soft or Desperate," *People's World* (San Francisco) (January 27, 1943), p. 5 U.

17 "Faulkneresque," *TLS* (October 10, 1942), p. 497.

18 Warren Beck, "A Note on Faulkner's Style," *Rocky Mountain Review*, 6 (Spring–Summer, 1942), pp. 5–6, 14; Cleanth Brooks, "What Deep South Literature Needs," *Saturday Review* (September 19, 1942), pp. 8–9, 29–30.

19 Conrad Aiken, "William Faulkner: The Novel as Form," *Atlantic Monthly*, 164 (November 1939), pp. 650–654; George Marion O'Donnell, "Faulkner's Mythology," *Kenyon Review*, 1 (Summer 1939), pp. 285–299; Delmore Schwartz, "The Fiction of William Faulkner," *Southern Review*, 7 (Summer 1941), pp. 145–160.

20 Michael Millgate, "William Faulkner: The Problem of Point of View," in *William Faulkner: Four Decades of Criticism*, ed. Linda Welshimer Wagner [Wagner-Martin] (East Lansing: Michigan State University Press, 1973), p. 179.

21 William Faulkner, *Go Down, Moses* (New York: Random House, 1942; Vintage edition, 1973), p. 3. Hereafter cited in text.

22 Coldfield, as Ellen and Rosa's father, becomes a central figure in *Absalom, Absalom!* His acceptance of Sutpen enabled the outsider's most blatant affront to the community, marrying one of its virgins. The fact that the eminently scrupled Coldfield finds Sutpen less objectionable than does the rest of the town (judging from the community's behavior at the wedding) raises serious questions about Coldfield's morality and makes his economic motives plausible. Is he consciously trading his older daughter for financial profits to his store?

The paucity of information about the Coldfields at the time of Sutpen's courtship does not balance the plethora of information Faulkner provides once Ellen is dead; by that time, he is telling Rosa's story (as Ellen's sister and, in a sense, her heir) rather than Sutpen's. In this back-and-fill narrative pattern, the reader benefits from seeing the demise of the mad father, Coldfield, who believes he can absolve himself of all responsibility for his family, business, and community by blocking out – literally hiding from – the Civil War. Coldfield not only abandons his role as father but becomes a child, demanding sustenance from his younger daughter. With utter disdain for his fatherly responsibility, Coldfield walls himself in his attic, leaving Rosa to secure food and bring it to him. It is chiefly as uncaring fathers that Faulkner draws – and damns – both

Coldfield and Sutpen. On this theme, see both Joseph A. Boone, "Paternal Narrative, Sexual Anxiety, and the Deauthorizing Designs of *Absalom, Absalom!*" (pp. 209–237) and Minrose C. Gwin, "(Re)Reading Faulkner as Father and Daughter of His Own Text" (pp. 238–258) in *Refiguring the Father, New Feminist Readings of Patriarchy*, eds. Patricia Yaeger and Beth Kowaleski-Wallace (Carbondale: Southern Illinois University Press, 1989). Of relevance, too, is Jay Martin's "Faulkner's 'Male Commedia': The Triumph of Manly Grief" in *Faulkner and Psychology*, Faulkner and Yoknapatawpha, 1991, eds. Donald M. Kartiganer and Ann J. Abadie (Jackson: University Press of Mississippi, 1994), pp. 123–164.

23 Ike's role in the novel has been one focus of recent controversy. After decades of being seen as noble in his relinquishment, a man who withstood the crass materialism of his peers, Ike was reappraised by such critics as Louis D. Rubin, Jr., who suggested in the 1980s that his withdrawal was harmful, little more than "a retreat from involvement" ("The Dixie Special: William Faulkner and the Southern Renaissance" in *Faulkner and the Southern Renaissance*, Faulkner and Yoknapatawpha, 1981, eds. Doreen Fowler and Ann J. Abadie [Jackson: University Press of Mississippi, 1982], p. 88). Judith Lockyer (*Ordered by Words, Language and Narration in the Novels of William Faulkner* [Carbondale: Southern Illinois University Press, 1991], p. 114) points out that Ike has at least taken the issue of patrimony seriously, rather than just accepting his role.

24 Or the reading of it; see David Wyatt's "Faulkner and the Reading Self" in *Faulkner and Psychology*, eds. Donald M. Kartiganer and Ann J. Abadie (Jackson: University Press of Mississippi, 1994), pp. 272–287.

25 Michael Millgate, *The Achievement of William Faulkner* (New York: Random House, 1966), p. 201; see also Millgate in *William Faulkner: Four Decades of Criticism*, p. 188. Thadious Davis elaborates on the place of *Go Down, Moses* in *Faulkner's "Negro": Art and the Southern Context* (Baton Rouge: Louisiana State University Press, 1983), pp. 239, 244.

26 As a monument to one man's arcane pride, Sutpen's Hundred brought corruption to a wilderness that might better have stayed the natural haven it was. Rather than benefiting from its existence, the community instead learned corruption – slavery, physical violence, cock fights, the interracial combat that made Sutpen and his African blacks equal.

Yet, because Sutpen's creation of his plantation was apparently

18

motivated by the same conventions as those of his successful, better placed, neighbors, people such as Colonel Compson not only dealt with him, they befriended him. The male quest for power which Sutpen's project illustrated was in no way foreign to these sons and grandsons of the founding fathers of the South. In their equation, the accumulation of wealth (here, land and house) equaled success, and eventually, social acceptability.

27 As did Cleanth Brooks in *William Faulkner: The Yoknapatawpha Country* (New Haven: Yale University Press, 1963), p. 244.

28 Nicole Moulineux, "The Enchantments of Memory: Faulkner and Proust" in *Faulkner, His Contemporaries, and His Posterity*, ed. Waldemar Zacharasiewicz (Tubingen: A. Francke Verlag, 1993), pp. 36–37.

29 Richard H. King, "Memory and Tradition" in *Faulkner and the Southern Renaissance*, pp. 138, 156, 152.

30 Somewhat more dated than the books by Creighton and Kuyk, Early's study persists in reading *Go Down, Moses* as a collection of stories of "charmingly benevolent whites and an all but comic old black woman." It follows from this interpretation that Early thinks Faulkner guilty of a "general sentimentalization of interracial relationships" (*The Making of Go Down, Moses* [Dallas: Southern Methodist University Press, 1972]), pp. 98–99.

31 Philip M. Weinstein, *Faulkner's Subject, A Cosmos No One Owns* (New York: Cambridge University Press, 1992), p. 43.

32 Wesley Morris with Barbara Alverson Morris, *Reading Faulkner* (Madison: University of Wisconsin Press, 1989), p. 231.

33 Mick Gidley, "Sam Fathers's Fathers: Indians and the Idea of Inheritance" in *Critical Essays on William Faulkner: The McCaslin Family*, ed. Arthur F. Kinney (Boston: G. K. Hall, 1990), p. 122.

34 James A. Snead, *Figures of Division: William Faulkner's Major Novels* (New York: Methuen, 1986), p. 180.

35 Daniel Hoffman, *Faulkner's Country Matters: Folklore and Fable in Yoknapatawpha* (Baton Rouge: Louisiana State University Press, 1989), p. 136; Albert J. Devlin, "History, Sexuality, and the Wilderness in the McCaslin Family Chronicle" in *Critical Essays on William Faulkner: The McCaslin Family*, p. 189.

36 Leon Forrest, "Faulkner/Reforestation" in *Faulkner and Popular Culture*, Faulkner and Yoknapatawpha, 1988, eds. Doreen Fowler and Ann J. Abadie (Jackson: University Press of Mississippi, 1990), pp. 212–213.

37 Myra Jehlen, *Class and Character in Faulkner's South* (New York:

19

Columbia University Press, 1976), pp. 104, 102; Diane Roberts, *Faulkner and Southern Womanhood* (Athens: University of Georgia Press, 1994), pp. 82, 49. See also Lee Jenkins, *Faulkner and Black-White Relations: A Psychoanalytic Approach* (New York: Columbia University Press, 1981).

38 Judith Lockyer, *Ordered by Words, Language and Narration in the Novels of William Faulkner,* p. 121.

39 Carolyn Porter, "Symbolic Fathers and Dead Mothers: A Feminist Approach to Faulkner" in *Faulkner and Psychoanalysis,* pp. 80, 111.

40 Philip M. Weinstein, *Faulkner's Subject, A Cosmos No One Owns* (New York: Cambridge University Press, 1992), p. 58.

41 Elisabeth Muhlenfeld, "The Distaff Side: The Women of *Go Down, Moses*" in *Critical Essays on William Faulkner: The McCaslin Family,* pp. 199, 210, 205.

42 Michael Grimwood, *Heart in Conflict: Faulkner's Struggles with Vocation* (Athens: University of Georgia Press, 1987), pp. 261, 267.

43 Eric J. Sundquist, *Faulkner: The House Divided* (Baltimore: Johns Hopkins University Press, 1983), pp. 153–154.

44 Karl F. Zender, *The Crossing of the Ways, William Faulkner, the South, and the Modern World* (New Brunswick, NJ: Rutgers University Press, 1989), pp. 65–69.

2

Touching Race in *Go Down, Moses*

JOHN T. MATTHEWS

OF all Faulkner's major works, *Go Down, Moses* remains the one most beset by anomaly and least certain of its place. Indisputably still the product of a master – emphatically so in the descriptions of the wilderness hunts – it nonetheless anticipates, particularly in Isaac McCaslin's convoluted defense of southern racial gradualism, Faulkner's long losing battles against the impotence of southern moderation on social issues, and against the garrulity that often overtakes his later style. Appearing six years after Faulkner had published perhaps the greatest of all American novels, *Go Down, Moses* searches out the contemporary consequences of what *Absalom, Absalom!* had already identified as the South's doom: That it was "now paying the price for having erected its economic edifice not on the rock of stern morality but on the shifting sands of opportunism and moral brigandage" (209). What does Ike's ascetic renunciation of social responsibility and his retreat to the big woods add to Quentin Compson's catatonic rehearsal of flawed design and his grief stricken plunge into oblivion?

What, too, are we to make of a work that presents itself as generically and formally unstable: a book *not* of short stories, as Faulkner insisted after the first edition's mistaken subtitle, but certainly not the unified novel he always claimed it to be? After the grand architecture of *Absalom*, the adroit short forms of *The Unvanquished* (1937), and the ingenious double plotting of *The Wild Palms* (1939), *Go Down, Moses* hesitates before a complexity that seems to overwhelm it. Its centerpiece, "The Bear," has acquired legendary stature as a *tour de force*, but perversely survives in two versions: one without the intricate disquisition on southern history in section 4, published separately as a short story within days of the publication of the second, the five-section version appearing in the "novel." The seven stories, whose thematic materials are interwoven (at least in the abundant criticism), remain tangential to each other; they touch without coalescing, leaving the abiding impression that they formalize a partially incoherent social scene. With the final dismantling of a plantocratic agriculture during the New Deal, with the South's long-delayed commitment to mechanization and commercial development by the late thirties, and with early telling blows against southern segregationism during World War II, much of what had made Faulkner's world did look unintelligible.

So might the uncertainty effect of *Go Down, Moses* be rationalized, but it may be possible to detect deeper purposes in a textual arrangement marked by anomaly, disjunction, parallax. It is fitting that the weakest, shortest, and least related of the seven stories gives the whole work its title. As if insisting on the centrality of its marginal situation, "Go Down, Moses" introduces a new character, Gavin Stevens, to oversee the last rites of a new protagonist, Samuel Worsham "Butch" Beauchamp. The reader, suffering something of a cognitive displacement from the world of the hunting stories preceding this one, may recall earlier strains as he or she moved from the frontier comedy of antebellum manners in "Was," through the moonshinery of "The Fire and the Hearth," to the bitter pathos of a lost lover's lynching in "Pantaloon," and finally into the august but remote magnificence of wilderness blood rituals in the hunting trilogy. At each of these points of transition, whether between stories or within them (consider the removes to the commissary for talk between rifle shots or to the sheriff's kitchen after Rider's murder), we confront a measure of disorientation. Only the slender threads of genealogical descent, stretched to the breaking point, or the compulsive permutations of ritualized violence, varied to the point of caricature, organize our transit.

Though a stranger to the narrative, Gavin Stevens appears to know the community represented so well that he can summon the work's master terms to achieve resolution. As he enlists the newspaper editor and other white townsmen to contribute to the expenses of Butch's return and funeral, he inspires a last show of paternalism. Indulging Miss Worsham's inadequate patronage of Mollie's requirement that her grandson find a proper end, Stevens pays for the privilege of ideological exercise. He insists that the whole white community subscribe to the project of "bring[ing] a dead nigger home" (360). Their generosity protects the lawyer and editor from seeing the traces of more profound social strain: Why is it only "by pure chance" that whites discover familiar blacks to be "brothers and sisters," and why should Hamp Worsham be "belly-bloated from the vegetables" (361) his household lives on during the Depression? Butch's execution in Joliet for murdering a policeman confirms Stevens' belief that he is just "the bad son of a bad father" (357), the South's obsession with blood and genealogy, with the "seed not only violent but dangerous and bad" (355), making this last Beauchamp the concluding sacrificial victim to the South's culture of racial violence: "the slain wolf" (364). Yet the lawyer's trope does not lay Butch's menace wholly to rest. As Eric Sundquist demonstrates, *Go Down, Moses* exhausts itself trying to perform the hunting ritual as an adequate sublimation of slavery's blood-mad bloodletting.

Stevens' accommodation of Butch's life through the ideology of paternalistic blood superiority, like Miss Worsham's assurance that the grief belongs only to the family, segregates a story that deserves freer circulation. Mollie's keening chant, which Stevens finds impenetrable to his comprehension and correction, firmly maintains another interpretation of her grandson's tragedy. By describing Butch's fate biblically, as another instance of a native son's betrayal into bondage by his own family, Mollie activates a discursive tradition of critical historical resonance. Not only does the slave gospel "Go Down Moses" situate Butch as yet another casualty of racial captivity, it also underscores the economic interests that compound race relations. Mollie insists that Roth Edmonds has "sold" her Benjamin to Pharaoh. If we look behind Stevens' account of Butch's malformed beginnings, we may grant that she has a point.

We learn that Butch has been exiled to Jefferson from Edmonds' plantation for breaking into the commissary. Having "spent a year in and out of jail for gambling and fighting," he goes to prison for robbing a store and assaulting an officer; death row finally claims him for killing another policeman in Chicago. The census taker who questions him finds his "black, smooth" face "impenetrable" (351), and he remains a cipher to both Stevens and the reader. Yet Butch's flashy "Hollywood" clothes, straightened hair, and ambition ("Getting rich too fast" [352]) mark his wolfishness as something more than the black beastliness rampant in racist fiction and popular culture.[1] Economically, Butch looks to be white, and triggers a series of crises by his will to trespass and steal. That a black in his position might believe himself entitled to the contents of the commissary, given the centuries of labor and life stolen from his ancestors, could well produce the hysterical moment of his first arrest, Butch "cursing through his broken mouth, his teeth fixed into something like furious laughter through the blood" (354). Black blood has been spilled in defense of the master's property, as it has been from time eternal through slavery. Butch's broken mouth hardly knows what to say, but speaking for him may be Mollie's elliptical indictment of Roth's updated practice of bondage. Once white landowners began accepting federal subsidies for crop reduction, which they refused to share proportionally with their tenants, were they not selling out their black labor?[2]

Mollie's request that the newspaper print Butch's story in its entirety – "all of hit" (365) – rests on some impulsion to see that the outlines of Butch's victimization appear alongside his dead body. More than just wanting things done right, or done white, Mollie wants Butch's story made public – not for herself, since she cannot read, and not to whitewash her grandson, since the editor believes she is willing to have even his shameful crime reported, but so that the record exists. In a novel so vastly dedicated to telling the stories of racism's casualties, to reading between the lines its mangled and cryptic evidence, from Eunice's suicide to Roth Edmonds disinheriting her infant descendant a century and a half later, Mollie gestures toward an author's determination to get this doubly interpretable story onto paper.[3]

Butch Beauchamp typifies one fate for the underenfranchised

black youth of the South. Racketeers in northern cities like Chicago drew easily impressed rural newcomers into numbers running, an apparently glamorous if dangerous route to quick money (Myrdal 330–332). Rackets flourished in black neighborhoods because there were so few legitimate economic opportunities. Underworld organizations accrued rudimentary financial clout, and even minimal political power in dealing with corrupt white politicians. Playing the numbers also expressed frustration with the long deferral of black enrichment. Slavery proper took a people for everything; the wage slavery that succeeded it merely robbed them blind. Being black under such economic regimes means being poor; to want more would always mean "getting rich too fast."

The meaning of Butch's story inheres in its marginal status. All but forgotten and discarded by the South that has produced him, he hides under an alias until the last moment, when a census taker seeks to number him with the rest. Like Richard Wright's Bigger Thomas, whose reluctant answers to a Northern questioner reveal a similarly scarred Mississippi past, Butch constitutes the image of the black that whites refuse to acknowledge as of their own making. Yet in silent tribute to the meaning of his life, a surprising number of townfolk assemble to greet Beauchamp's return home, "Negroes and whites both," with "half a hundred Negroes, men and women too, watching quietly" (363).

By lingering over such incidental moments, in an apparently anticlimactic story, I propose a way of reading *Go Down, Moses* that seeks to discern Faulkner's studied conviction that economic exploitation and racial oppression composed a double coil around the modern South. Rather than sacrifice either economics or race for the purposes of analysis, I propose a kind of double reading that demonstrates their mutual constitution.

Faulkner's grasp of the interdependence of economic and racial injustice coincides with Gunnar Myrdal's "theory of the vicious circle" to account for the plight of the Negro in America (Myrdal 75). Though the vast collective work of sociology published in 1944 as *An American Dilemma* elaborated the economic consequences of nearly every feature of black subordination in the United States, Myrdal was careful not to reduce the peculiar disadvantaged status of Negroes to that of other underclasses. He rejected "the idea that there is *one* predominant factor, a 'basic factor' " (Myrdal 77) that could explain the "pathological" (Myrdal 205) economic condition of blacks in America. Rather than rely on such "economic determinism" (Myrdal 77), Myrdal and his team sought to assess the more subtle ways in which causes turned to effects, and effects to further causes. In "an interdependent system of dynamic causation" (Myrdal 78), multiple factors mattered; "the Negro's legal and political status," "considerations by whites of social prestige, and everything else in the Negro problem belong to the causation of discrimination in the labor market" (Myrdal 78). Both the representation of race in the cultural sphere and the practice of race relations in the social sphere influence economic arrangements as much as they are influenced by them.[4]

The doubled perspectives of *Go Down, Moses* realize these complex relations. At one moment in Isaac and Cass's dialogue over the South, the parallax of Faulkner's imaginative method produces the sought effect. After recounting the crimes of passion and property marring old Carothers' husbandry, the cousins agree the land is "cursed." In the following passage, the plantation must be apprehended severally as a site of conflicted labor, production, race, and genealogy – each realized in terms of the other:

"Cursed:" and again McCaslin merely lifted one hand, not even speaking and not even toward the ledgers: so that, as the stereopticon condenses into one instantaneous field the myriad minutia of its scope, so did that slight and rapid gesture establish in the small cramped and cluttered twilit room not only the ledgers but the whole plantation in its mazed and intricate entirety – the land, the fields and what they represented in terms of cotton ginned and sold, the men and women whom they fed and clothed and even paid a little cash money at Christmas-time in return for the labor which planted and raised and picked and ginned the cotton, the machinery and mules and gear with which they raised it and their cost and upkeep and replacement – that whole edifice intricate and complex and founded upon injustice and erected by ruthless rapacity and carried on even yet with at times downright savagery not only to the human beings but the valuable animals too, yet solvent and efficient and, more than that: not only still intact but enlarged, increased; brought still intact by McCaslin, himself little more than a child then, through and out of the debacle and chaos of twenty years ago where hardly one in ten survived, and enlarged and increased and would continue so, solvent and efficient and intact and still increasing so long as McCaslin and his McCaslin successors lasted, even though their surnames might not even be Edmonds then: and he: "Habet too. Because that's it: not the land, but us. Not only the blood, but the name too; not only its color but its designation." (284–285)

Stereopticons create one of two effects. They may cause an image to blur gradually into a second image. This is the kind of serial resolution a reading of either race or economics as "basic factor" might achieve. One set of features may be tracked back to its founding cause in either the psychopathology of southern racism or capitalist expropriation of common wealth (in the joint properties of slave labor and the land itself). But the stereoptical effect described above involves a "condensation" of particles, one that organizes the image within a field and gives it dimensionality. Through such effects, Faulkner may describe a world in which "blood," "name," and "color," like "labor," "land," and "return," can be apprehended only in "intricate entirety."

If we contemplate the strain of holding mutually contributory social factors in mind simultaneously, we may freshly appreciate Faulkner's stylistic contortions here and elsewhere. According to the usual explanation, Faulkner's celebrated ambition to put all "between one Cap and period" involves the conviction that the past is a part of every moment and individual, making, as Faulkner himself put it, "the long sentence . . . an attempt to get his past and possibly his future into the instant in which he does something" (*Faulkner in the University* 84). In the passage above, one grants the style's temporality – its diachronic vector – as a function of historicity; the edifice founded on injustice and rapacity survives into the present, implicating Ike and Cass as products of that history. At the same time, this extended sentence assembles – synchronically – the "myriad minutia" [sic] of the whole plantation system. It touches upon the terms of labor dependency, suggesting that the inequity of tenancy doubles the

27

"injustice" of slavery. It notes the legerdemain ruling a train of unfaithful "representations": labor spent is reduced to cotton ginned, cotton sold to costs discharged. It compounds the habit of "savagery" toward inferior species with the vigilance over surnames, property rights, and succession. All in all, the sentence performs an act of descriptive analysis in which the plantation South resolves as a complex image of mutual causes. Articulated singly, the question of race may obscure that of economics; condensed, the causes compose a dimensional discourse.[5] Such an approach organizes Myrdal's model of "cumulative causation" (77); it is as if Faulkner has already developed the stylistic and structural means to render the problem artistically.

One structural consequence of a "stereoptical aesthetics" appears in the *narrative* repetitiveness of Go Down, Moses. It is true that the compulsion to repeat in Faulkner's texts amounts to a symptomology: of oedipal mourning (Irwin), of racial obsession (Sundquist), of self-revisionism (Moreland). Yet in their less mesmeric moments, Faulkner's replayed scenes allow slight discrepancies to produce significance through bivalence. The scene of Butch's apprehension in "Go Down, Moses," for example, recalls the conclusion of "Pantaloon in Black," when the maddened Rider is finally borne down under the weight of his fellow prisoners. The deputy finds him lying on the floor, "laughing, with tears big as glass marbles running across his face and down past his ears and making a kind of popping sound on the floor like somebody dropping bird eggs, laughing and laughing and saying, 'Hit look lack Ah just cant quit thinking. Look lack Ah just cant quit' " (154). Rider and Butch meet in the same moment of helpless hysteria, their lives reduced to futility.

Though Rider and Butch begin and end alike, their lives describe inverted arcs. Coevals on the Edmonds plantation (Butch tells the census taker he is 26 [352], Rider is 24 [133]), both start dangerously. Rider, too, takes to dice, whiskey, and women – until another life altogether beckons him. When he sees Mannie for the "first time," after knowing her all his life, Rider renounces the legacy of shiftlessness assigned him as a black in the thirties South. Rider shows no interest in farming – sensibly, since by 1940 virtually all tenants had been driven from the land. The roaming timberman strides "across the slope" of "old abandoned fields upon the hills" (138). Nor has he been reduced to the bare subsistence of wage-earning family men. For the brief bright moment of Rider and Mannie's marriage, this southern black couple enjoy relative economic enfranchisement and a taste of subclass mobility. The story celebrates the wedding of labor and profit, of industry and thrift, of self-denial and fulfillment. Mannie's domestic grace teams with Rider's triumph as salaried worker, his personal might waged to master nature's "primal inertia," her vision sanctifying financial ascent. Mannie and Rider buy their way into the commissary Butch breaks into. Faulkner indulges his own fantasy of the black who earns his way to freedom and equality.[6]

Yet payday's ritual of presentation and consumption, which translates labor into goods and even love, ends prematurely and unintelligibly for the black wage slave of the modernizing South. With Mannie's unexplained death, Rider loses his purchase on a life of betterment. He acts out his lost bearings by caricaturing both his future work (turning the biggest log ever, then quitting) and his renounced past (swallowing the bust-skull whiskey, then gagging). But the "silvering, glinting" column of liquor, like the "silver solid air" (144) through which he plunges, cannot replace "the bright cascade of silver dollars onto the scrubbed table" (134).

Mannie haunts "Pantaloon in Black" as the phantom of unrealized social and economic entitlement. She represents a life for southern blacks first deferred and then denied. Without having "done" anything, she simply vanishes, her absence suggesting indirectly the space of equality foreclosed by white vigilance. Rider does not know what to strike at in his grief and rage, but he finds his way to a scene representative of his woes. Finally reading the "signs" right, he finds the white "boss-man"'s game and calls the night watchman for cheating at dice with "miss-outs." Birdsong's hand must be sprung open – if only to reveal that black "boys" cannot win. Rider finds that seeking justice provokes lethal conflict. The cotton string looping his neck also suspends his razor, until he brings it "forward" and "free[s]" it. However, no sacrificial union redeems either Birdsong's slit throat or Rider's lynching; wilderness rituals will not cover this carnage, cannot promise that mortal combatants will work through to respect and love. The ex-timberman turns one last time "so that not even the first jet of blood touched his hand or arm" (149), just as his anonymous murderers want nothing to do with his forsaken body. Violence performs blood segregation; social prohibitions against touch guard against equal competition. Rider's disciplined body has been remanded to the negro schoolhouse, where it is left to proclaim the only lesson worth learning.

One contaminant, however, persists in Yoknapatawpha's segregated white space: discourse itself. To his wife, the deputy tries out his account of Rider's behavior as simply subhuman, though he senses that racial ways cannot fully explain Rider's bizarre end. Insisting that Rider's apparent refusal to grieve proves he "aint human," the deputy never thinks to ask what the totality of Rider's behavior declares about him. Losing his prospects and giving up his job, Rider crosses the "junctureless backloop of time's trepan" (147) by acting out his entrapment in historically inescapable forms of peonage (given the South's refusal to address political, social, economic, and educational grievances). Jailed, Rider sees his "timber gang" (147) replaced by "the chain gang" (153), a reminder that the South's economy long depended on the labor supplied by prisoners to private leasers.[7] Finally, lynched, Rider stands witness to the modern South's worst lingering shame. These signs of Rider's meaning within the economics of race jeopardize all efforts to reduce him to anomaly. The deputy's wife understands this better perhaps than her husband. When he proposes that she "take" the example of Rider to prove his theory of black subhumanity, she replies: "I wish you would. . . . Take him out of my kitchen, anyway" (150). It is the spectral trespassings authorized by imaginative discourse that threaten the security of white enclaves and prepare for the unthinkable. When blacks are invited into the kitchen – for other reasons than Dilsey's, and for longer stays than Joe Christmas's – whites might begin to hear from blacks on what they both have missed out.[8]

The only black with economic stature on Edmonds' plantation is Lucas Beauchamp. For good reason Mannie and Rider model their marriage on that of their elder neighbors, even imitating their emblematic fire on the hearth. Though Mannie's death ought to have ended Rider's hopes, he marvels, as the chain gang fells him, that he just "cant quit thinking" (154). Lucas may indulge similar thoughts of prosperity as he patiently builds his bank account, takes custody of his older brother's unclaimed bequest from his white ancestors, cultivates a thriving trade in corn liquor, and indifferently meets his landlord's demands for increased productivity that will mean nothing to the laborer's profit. Having been granted his plot of land in the middle of the "family" plantation, Lucas takes pride in the slight advantage he has over the usual black tenant farmer: he is freer, "plowing and planting and working it when and how he saw fit (or maybe not even doing that, maybe sitting through a whole morning on his front gallery, looking at it and thinking if that's what he felt like doing)" (35–36). Read against Rider's, Lucas's thinking may unify around his lifelong effort to compensate himself for the state of dispossession into which he has been born.

It is not only that Lucas cares a good deal about money, tempted though the reader may be to dismiss his exploits as harmless tomfoolery.[9] More important, Lucas relies on an ideology of economic self-realization to formulate his response to the very practices that have put him where he is. When the Indian burial mound spits its single coin of potential indemnification, Lucas does not so much abandon his life as intensify it. His moonshining must be recognized as a longstanding recourse of the southern poor. Especially in mountain regions, where lumber and coal industries collapsed as the Depression began, but elsewhere throughout the region, Prohibition expanded the market that southern state regulations outlawing liquor had already created (Kirby 205). (Southern states maintained liquor controls before and after the federal Volstead Act [Kirby 206].) All moonshiners ran great risk, but especially blacks, given the authority local deputies possessed in hunting contraband stills and liquor. Lucas persists with moonshining for the same reason Roth opposes it; cash supplements loosened tenants' thralldom to the farms of their landlords. Roth may be particularly annoyed with Lucas's underproduction in 1940 because the war was raising cotton prices.

Having enough money in the bank to last his lifetime turns out to be no more satisfactory to Lucas than it must have been to old Carothers or any other planter under southern capitalism. As he waits for George and Nat to clear the scene for his hunt, Lucas worries that he may not live long enough "not only to find the treasure but to get any benefit and pleasure from it" (73). Lucas associates the stroke that will make him "rich" (60) with the establishment of his independence from farming. As he waits for his chance to begin his search for Buck and Buddy's "buried money," he notes that the "abeyance" coincides with the suspension of labor, "the good year, the good early season, and cotton and corn springing up almost in the planter's wheel-print, so that there was now nothing to do but lean on the fence and watch it grow" (73). Should Lucas find the treasure, he contemplates the resumption of his cropping ("something to occupy him" [60]) or its loss ("he was a little sorry to give up farming" [42]) with equanimity. The circuit of ancestral wealth and sharecropping yields the spectacle of one slave descendant recovering a token of the plantation riches that derive from the buried value of first slave, then tenant, labor.

Lucas's schemes of enrichment accord with his general method of dealing with his Edmonds past. Repeatedly in his literal and symbolic negotiations with that legacy, Lucas attempts to undo or equalize the economic harm done him. In his petty financial skirmishes with Roth, as in pressuring him to advance money for the metal detector, as well as in more symbolically reverberant actions, like kidnapping Alice Ben Bolt, whose value derives from a condemned agricultural order and whose price ($300) matches the amount paid for his mother by the McCaslin twins, Lucas keeps an eye on the debit column. His ledger mentality, if you will, presides over every challenge he mounts to his dispossession. When, most spectacularly, he confronts Zack Edmonds over the expropriation of his wife, Lucas explains the psychic economy of his suicidal mission:

You knowed I could beat you, so you thought to beat me with old
Carothers, like Cass Edmonds done Isaac. . . . And you thought I'd do
that too, didn't you? You thought I'd do it quick, quicker than Isaac
since it aint any land I would give up. I aint got any fine big McCaslin
farm to give up. All I got to give up is McCaslin blood that rightfully aint
even mine or at least aint worth much since old Carothers never seemed
to miss much what he give to Tomey that night that made my father.
(55–56)

But Lucas won't give up the little he possesses. And had he
evened the score by taking out Zack, he would not have killed
himself: *"I would have paid. So I reckon I aint got old Carothers' blood
for nothing, after all"* (57).

Such a metaphorics of racial equality indicates a conceptual
dilemma. How does the object of subjugation imagine and attain
freedom within a social discourse founded on his or her domination? After *Absalom, Absalom!* Faulkner ups the ante in *Go Down,
Moses* by tracing the South's tragedy beyond the particular mal-
formation of New World capitalist slavocracy to the principle of
domination inherent in Western civilization's mastery over nature. In "The Concept of Enlightenment," Horkheimer and
Adorno argue that the key steps in the imaginative and later
material control of nature involve primitive peoples' development of conceptual practices such as substitution, repetition, and
abstraction. Myth emerges as a set of symbol-making equiva-
lences, subduing the contingency of natural event by subjecting
it to the will of a universal spirit and to the performance of
ritual. Later, rational enlightenment comes to supplant mythical
thought, but Horkheimer and Adorno insist on their continued
relationship: "Myth turns into enlightenment, and nature into
mere objectivity. Men pay for the increase of their power with
alienation from that over which they exercise their power. Enlightenment behaves toward things as a dictator toward men"
(Horkheimer and Adorno 9).

Relations of power organize the conceptual domination of
nature just as they structure the operation of language: "Substitution in the course of sacrifice marks a step toward discursive
logic" (Horkheimer and Adorno 10). The same dynamic under-
girds the emergence of an exchange economy and the formation

of the bourgeois subject: "Bourgeois society is ruled by equivalence. It makes the dissimilar comparable by reducing it to abstract quantities" (7). Only by translating the value of dissimilar commodities into an arbitrary register that can mediate them (first as abstract proportions of each other, then as money) may goods be exchanged in the marketplace. As a result, products turn partially abstract and forfeit some of the value determined by labor spent and use gained. Hence the domination of nature and the formation of an exchange economy prove inseparable from the project of the subject's emancipation under Enlightenment. They all rest on the mechanics of value production – differentiation and abstraction. Here lies theoretical ground for Faulkner's entanglement with the mystery that the very language of freedom for the bourgeois social subject rests on the logic of enslavement.

Lucas seeks to enter and occupy the social arrangements that have been founded on his exclusion. Playing Roth like a slot machine, testing the bank's deposit and withdrawal apparatus, even getting a receipt for services purchased at the end of *Intruder in the Dust*, Lucas displays what it means for him to believe that old Carothers "come and spoke for me" (57). Already articulated, the social text conceptually depends on habits of domination. That Lucas resists by imitating his creator and dispossessor spells his doom, at the same time it grants him a measure of dignity:

> Yet it was not that Lucas made capital of his white or even his McCaslin blood, but the contrary. . . . He didn't even have to bother to defy it. He resisted it simply by being the composite of the two races which made him, simply by possessing it. Instead of being at once the battleground and victim of the two strains, he was a vessel, durable, ancestryless, nonconductive, in which the toxin and its anti stalemated one another. (101)

The historically *southern* version of the curse of domination appears in Lucas's contradictory position. He faces a legacy founded on his own disinheritance, a "ravaged patrimony" (284), a patrimony of ravishment. The critical mood in Faulkner's career that brings the confrontation with atrocity into focus extends through a decade of writing that exhibits one stunned witness after another – Quentin Compson, Gail Hightower, Isaac McCaslin. All suffer the shock of recognition that "the whole edifice intricate and complex [was] founded upon injustice and erected by ruthless rapacity and carried on even yet with at times downright savagery" (285). So little may be said after this, yet Isaac discovers that even saying "No" to it may be too much.

In an effort to flee patrimony and ravishment, Ike encounters their specters in the wilderness. Not just the touch of landowner's ax on the virginal forest, or the touch of master's hand on the slave's body, but the touch of instrumental reason on nature begins the train of corruption. One sees the history stretching in both directions: the regime of plantation and enslavement reaches back beyond white planters to their Chickasaw predecessors. The Great Buck that Sam Fathers salutes embodies the memory of those lost and sacrificed to the domestication of the wilderness – "Oleh, Chief, Grandfather," "as if it were walking out of the very sound of the horn which related its death" (177). Yet Sam's attempt to oppose genocidal history with blood ritual exposes their similarity. The Chickasaws' rites of power leave them with hands no less bloody than those of the European settlers who eventually supplant them. Ike's learning to "spill the blood he loves" marks him with the achievement of mastery over nature; it distills the essential relationship of human to nature through domination. "Every attempt to break the natural thralldom, because nature is broken, enters all the more deeply into that natural enslavement. Hence the course of European civilization. Abstraction, the tool of enlightenment, treats its objects as did fate, the notion of which it rejects: it liquidates them" (Horkheimer and Adorno 13).

The legacy of domination structures the present use of the wilderness as well. Though Ike imagines leaving history behind when he enters the "nothing" of the wilderness – like shutting off talk about Hitler by concentrating on the need to make camp (323) – the woods crawl with reminders that they suppress and so re-embody the social matter left behind. Recall the assertion that the "best" of the hunts begin and end in talk, a talk quartered "in the libraries of town houses or the offices of plantation houses" (184). The annual rites emanate from the needs of leading landowners like de Spain and Compson and Edmonds. Their retinue includes a guide (Sam), a marksman (Ewell), an aide-de-camp (Boon), and a black domestic staff (Tennie and Ash); camp arrangements thus reinscribe a society of privilege. Ash's late complaint about his exclusion from the things that matter, though dismissed comically, amplifies the barely audible exercise of domination in the woods. When de Spain thinks (wrongly) that Ben has jumped one of his colts, he finds the right language to express his concerns: "But now he has come into my house and destroyed my property, out of season too. He broke the rules" (205).

Shocking as has been Ike's discovery in the commissary ledgers of old Carothers' moral atrocity, he reels under one further act of treachery. The year after Old Ben and Sam Fathers die, he visits Major de Spain's office in Jefferson to ask permission to return to the camp. Ike knows that the hunt will never be the same; the deaths of his coevals point to the dwindling span of his life and that of the woods themselves. He has learned that de Spain has sold the timber rights to the land they used, but when he sees his hunting elder in his place of business Ike cannot at first make a double image resolve:

the boy standing there looking down at the short plumpish grey-haired man in sober fine broadcloth and an immaculate glazed shirt whom he was used to seeing in boots and muddy corduroy; unshaven, sitting the shaggy powerful long-hocked mare with the worn Winchester carbine across the saddlebow and the great blue dog standing motionless as bronze at the stirrup, the two of them in that last year and to the boy anyway coming to resemble one another somehow as two people competent for love or for business who have been in love or in business together for a long time sometimes do. (303)

Eventually Ike's train of thought finds the stereoptical whole: the hunter *is* the man of business. The sale confirms that the wilderness has been – for longer than they, in mind as in deed – property.

Should not the last cry ringing from the woods recall the first? "Get out of here! Dont touch them! Dont touch a one of them!

They're mine!" (315). Boon, frantically assembling his shotgun, wards off competition:

At first glance the tree seemed to be alive with frantic squirrels. There appeared to be forty or fifty of them leaping and darting from branch to branch until the whole tree had become one green maelstrom of mad leaves, while from time to time, singly or in twos and threes, squirrels would dart down the trunk then whirl without stopping and rush back up again as though sucked violently back by the vacuum of their fellows' frenzied vortex. (315)

Like the bear cub terrified by his first glimpse of the lumber train, the squirrels register the fatal touch of human possession. Faulkner's strategy of repetition expands the scene's significance, for it resembles Rider's last moment as well: "at last they pulled him down – a big mass of nigger heads and arms and legs boiling around on the floor and even then Ketcham says every now and then a nigger would come flying out and go sailing through the air across the room, spraddled out like a flying squirrel" (154). Adding Old Ben's demise compounds the cubist effect: Ike "could see Lion still clinging to the bear's throat and he saw the bear, half erect, strike one of the hounds with one paw and hurl it five or six feet and then . . . Boon was running . . . leap[ing] among the hounds, hurdling them, kicking them aside as he ran, and fling[ing] himself astride the bear" (230). Together these narrative sequences represent an historical palimpsest of deadly dispossession.

By prefacing the wilderness trilogy with a plantation trilogy, Faulkner brilliantly demonstrates the continuity of their logic. The opening stories establish the single discourse of farm and forest. The domestic versions of the wilderness ethos begin figuratively and so innocently: hunting Tomey's Turl as if he were a fox, hunting the fox as if he were a pet, trapping Uncle Buck as if he were an unwary hunter in "bear country." As has been well remarked, these forms darken in their course through Lucas's hunt for gold, his remembered baying of Zack over a contested wife, and finally the desperate slaying of a timberman amid scenes of the forest's destruction. On eventual arrival in the woods, the reader encounters a practice of blood sanctity, ritual sacrifice, fraternal exclusion, and historical denial that deeply stains the "Utopian" matter of wilderness ways.[10] Just before the aged Ike dreams a vision of "unaxed trees and sightless brakes where the strong immortal game ran forever" (337–338), he acknowledges that a "man had had to marry his planting to the wilderness in order to conquer it" (326). To plant is to conquer nature; to cultivate a plantation is to "translate" the wilderness; to make a profit, to commandeer labor; to exercise authority, to dominate the landless, slaves, women, and children (of whom, as Roth says, there is never a "scarcity" [323]).

Horkheimer and Adorno enable us to see that the southern instance conforms to the general condition. The brutality internal to the project of enlightenment – the violence inherent in abstraction and equivalence-making – makes southern racialist ideology, like an otherwise so different European fascism, a conceptual product of Western idealism. It is no wonder that in "Delta Autumn" the last strained determination to flee to the woods must negotiate a prefatory confrontation with the subject of Hitler, fascism, and demagoguery. Members of the hunting party awkwardly stumble over American reluctance to enter World War II in 1940 and to defeat the forces of modern statism at home. Products as they are of their own southern "savage ideal" (in W. J. Cash's memorable phrase), these "doe" and "coon" hunters are hardly in a position to challenge even an "Austrian paper-hanger" (323). One ideological problem for southern support of American participation in the war against Hitler involved race. How could a segregated society oppose Nazism's race-based social vision? Could a single morality justify lynching and condemn genocide (Myrdal 517)? Faulkner flushes this contradiction out of hiding when he has Uncle Ike identify an order overthrown:

This land which man has deswamped and denuded and derivered in two generations so that white men can own plantations and commute every night to Memphis and black men own plantations and ride in jim crow cars to Chicago to live in millionaires' mansions on Lakeshore Drive, where white men rent farms and live like niggers and niggers crop on shares and live like animals, where cotton is planted and grows man-tall in the very cracks of the sidewalks and usury and mortgage and bankruptcy and measureless wealth, Chinese and African and Aryan and Jew, all breed and spawn together until no man has time to say which one is which nor cares. (347)

Ike's racist condemnation of amalgamation confesses its economic basis in the smooth modulation of this passage. The derangements produced by government and business activities during the 1930s led to the neoplantation system that enriched investor masters. But Ike allows that explanation to drift toward a racialist account, one that, true to American form, mistakes class for race.

As a member of a southern white liberal intelligentsia, Faulkner struggled to imagine what the place for the enfranchised black subject would be. Suppose the ascent for blacks from slavery, peonage, and wage labor might involve some arrival in the bourgeoisie, a class only belatedly emerging for whites in the small town mercantile culture of the 1940s South. What would it mean only to substitute new content into a discredited conceptual and social apparatus? What would it mean that the very language and practice of freedom carried the curse of deep-seated habits of differentiation, stratification, and identity-through-exclusion?

It must be admitted that for Ike, as for many other white conservative opponents and moderate gradualists on southern race matters, such a tendency *toward* universalizing the problem always remains susceptible to being used to rationalize the status quo. Ike would like to put Roth's mistress off for "a long while" by sending her north to marry a black man. Faulkner counsels going slow, a call that grimly repeats a century and a half of white confidence in gradualism. And those intent as I am on describing the economic, social, and conceptual continuities between plantation agriculture under slavery and that under a cash economy (what Willis distinguishes as peripheral and semi-peripheral status), may be faulted for underestimating the differences produced by the undeniable transformation of the South in the 1930s. On the other hand, the nation's continued inability to resolve racial conflict, a condition worsening alarmingly now in the mid 1990s, argues for the intractability of racial problems in isolation from the conceptual and practical economics that help structure them. Put bluntly, as Enlightenment reason depends on anti-Semitism, according to Horkheimer and Adorno, so American capitalism depends on racism.

Faulkner's text almost manages to make a kind of Southern Agrarian critique of modern business culture touch a quite opposed liberal critique of southern racism. Such moments of profound cultural recognition, in which capitalism and race prove indivisible, stand as the primal scenes of *Go Down, Moses*. Conclusively, Ike's reading of the commissary ledgers reveals the valuation of tools, supplies, and human bodies promiscuously as forms of property. But well before the scene of Ike's moral initiation, Cass has witnessed its prefiguration. By the end of "Was," virtually every non-playing individual – slave and half-brother, sister, and brother – has been swept into the stakes of Buddy's and Hubert's poker game. The story insists that any body may be monetized by the master's decree.

The vertiginous poker game casts a spotlight on the plantation's unsustainable traffic in human chattel. The game's human stakes, though laughed off and "not called," traumatize the bidders. The calculus presiding over the evaluation and exchange of individuals confesses its own comic inadequacy:

"One hand," he said. "Draw. You shuffle, I cut, this boy deals. Five hundred dollars against Sibbey. And we'll settle this nigger business once and for all too. If you win, you buy Tennie; if I win, I buy that boy of yours. The price will be the same for each one: three hundred dollars."

"Win?" Uncle Buck said. "The one that wins buys the niggers?"

"Wins Sibbey, damn it!" Mr Hubert said. "Wins Sibbey! What the hell else are we setting up till midnight arguing about? The lowest hand wins Sibbey and buys the niggers." (23)

The bids escalate so steeply with every passing draw that the object of the game soon becomes extrication rather than victory.

As the emblem of slavery's trade in flesh – which commodifies everything it touches, from consanguinity to marriage – the story's "business" induces a kind of temporary amnesia. When Hubert and Buddy seem to agree on the final version of the bidding, they stop talking: "For about a minute it was like he and Uncle Buddy had both gone to sleep" (27). And when Lucas Beauchamp realizes that his own daughter has turned his methods of extortion against him, he blanks out: "He might have been asleep standing, as a horse sleeps" (67). These moments register a primary forgetfulness in all economic transactions: the forgetting of the particularities of the objects to be abstracted and equated. In the case of humans the attributes incommensurable to commodification prove all the more unthinkable.

According to a certain logic, all that proves incommensurable might return from its suppression under abstraction in the form of a claimant flesh, the body "itself." *Absalom, Absalom!* harbors this hope in its description of Clytie's hand laid in restraint of Rosa's trespassing: *"But let flesh touch with flesh, and watch the fall of all the eggshell shibboleth of caste and color too"* (112). Lodged deeply beneath discursive distortion may lie what Ike calls the one "truth [that] covers all things that touch the heart" (249). Based on a pre-rational, natural, and self-present truth, such a morality might well be expected to refute the abstract shibboleth of law.

The space opened by Faulkner's stereoptical aesthetics, however, refuses to be short-circuited by solutions imagined within the private heart, those constituted by the singular touch. Instead, the truth of the heart, as Myrdal understood, was the truth of collective belief, and that an egalitarian one: "The American Negro problem is a problem in the heart of the American. . . . Though our study includes economic, social, and political race relations, at bottom our problem is the moral dilemma of the American – the conflict between his moral valuations on various levels of consciousness and generality" (Myrdal xlvii). Show the material and social conditions at odds with the creed of American equality, Myrdal believed, and the solution of the "Negro question" would continue to advance. Display the embeddedness of social and economic forms in enlightenment abstraction, Faulkner's writing suggests, and the full dimensionality of the nation's racial burden comes into focus.

At the moment Ike McCaslin touches the hand of Roth's

41

mistress, he feels, despite himself, the thrill of his black kins-man's blood coursing under his own. Yet the sentimentality of this touching moment ought not deflate the novel's work of analysis. Ike's hand, it is true, rests on "the smooth young flesh where the strong old blood ran after its long lost journey back to home" (345). But since Tennie's Jim has lost patrimony, pa-tronym, and place, that flesh returns him to "home" only in the most abstract of forms, only as the socially dead equivalent of Butch Beauchamp. The young woman's hand entwined with Ike's may figure the mixture of blood that will finally make the southern family one, but the cash it holds still interleaves their clasp.

NOTES

1 Throughout his book, Sundquist discusses the intersection of Faulkner's fiction with a white southern imaginative tradition that represents blacks as beasts. He comments on this aspect of Go Down, Moses in particular conjunction with Thomas Dixon's novels (139–148).

2 Kirby summarizes: "The first stage in the consolidation of planta-tions was the wholesale eviction of tenants of all classes, especially sharecroppers. This process was protracted, but it seems to have been underway all over the South by 1934, the first full crop year following the creation of the AAA [Agricultural Adjustment Administration]" (64). On pre-Depression plantations, landlords showed some preference for black sharecroppers because their ra-cial subordination made them more compliant to unfavorable lease arrangements and to the intimidation used by landowners to pre-vent croppers from moving to more favorable conditions (Kirby 237).

3 John Carlos Rowe interprets this scene as an instance of Faulkner's confrontation with his own social and artistic limitations in repre-senting race in Go Down, Moses (81). Rowe argues that the short story sequence refuses the will to totalized form characteristic of the modernist polyvocal novel, and that this gesture signals Faulk-ner's recognition that received social forms like paternalism and the blood family must be replaced for African-Americans to be enfranchised with "the independent voices he knows they must

have in a truly 'New' South" (78). Though Rowe's article appeared too late for me to address the implications of his argument in the body of my essay, I note that in my judgment his view of modernism discounts its capacity for social critique, and that a work like *Go Down, Moses,* which according to Rowe "demonized his own literary authority" (93) by linking authorial control to social mastery, nonetheless contributed to the ideological shift that allowed liberal democratic principles to compel the South's desegregation.

4   In addition to the near simultaneity of Myrdal's study and Faulkner's novel (at a moment when the onset of World War II greatly escalated racial tensions), the works may be read as similar leading expressions of the hope that the ideals of liberal democracy could address the longstanding shame of American racism. According to David Southern, no book was more influential in shaping national policies to end segregation in the forties and fifties than *An American Dilemma.* Likewise, despite the present low regard for Faulkner's racial politics, his fiction was widely read in its time as decisively critical of the South's "closed society." Though both Myrdal (and his collaborators) and Faulkner saw the "question of the Negro" ultimately in terms of morality, that is of beliefs held consciously by individuals, each assiduously constructed accounts of racial status that deeply respected the power of historical conditioning. Myrdal's emphasis on economics, understandable given his and his collaborator Richard Sterner's academic specialization in economics, sought a specifically Southern explanation for the plight of the African-American. Myrdal refused a Marxian account of blacks as members of the proletariat, insisting that the peculiar history of slavery and a present-day racial caste system produced a distinctive set of conditions. Faulkner rarely receives credit for multivariable analysis of the question of race. Reading him against Myrdal lets us see how his fiction delineates an interplay of material and ideological factors, and how his art reproduces for closer attention the discursive realities of his world.

5   Sundquist brilliantly accounts for the white tradition of representing race in the American South, but he does not pursue the question of economic arrangements either as historical context or as represented material within the fiction he examines. Snead valuably demonstrates the self-deconstruction of racial binarism as Faulkner's texts reproduce it; his analysis is strictly discursive, though it seeks to comprehend textual and social manifestations of racial polarization. Philip Weinstein concentrates on Faulkner's

sympathies and limitations in representing the subjectivities of blacks and white women, giving us a meticulous description of Faulkner's efforts to imagine experience outside his own. My approach seeks to complicate these by suggesting a *relational* model that governs Faulkner's most ambitious efforts to render his world, and to complement the attention paid to his imagining subjectivity with an awareness of the discursive and economic practices defining the possibilities for self-constitution.

Conversely, the most instructive analyses of class, labor, and capital production in *Go Down, Moses* tend to see racial relations as an effect of economic ones. For example, Willis concludes her immensely useful analysis of economic dependency in "The Bear" by suggesting that the South's modern conversion from a peripheral to a semi-peripheral relationship to northern capital and industry produces a sense of community in which the empowered group defines "a dominant other (epitomized by the white Northern capitalist) and an inferior other (characterized by all degress [sic] of ethnicity)" (103). Perhaps as a result of a proper focus on the historical transition of the South from a regime of paternalistic slave-worked agriculture to one of market relations, Marxist analyses like Jehlen's, Godden's, and Willis's concentrate on the wilderness trilogy. The other four stories of the novel, however, dimensionalize the change in economic regime by suggesting the persistence of a racialized discourse within which such changes must be imagined and experienced, perhaps differently by different subjects.

Concentrating on "The Bear," as Willis and, to a lesser extent, Godden do, also produces an exaggerated estimate of Ike's resemblance to Faulkner. Though Faulkner never violated white racial custom in his personal life, there is no question but that his fiction occupied much more progressive ground. It is worth remembering that James Silver invited him to a meeting of southern sympathizers with the civil rights movement in Mississippi's "closed society" (and that he went), and that Myrdal lists him with Erskine Caldwell, Paul Green, Ellen Glasgow, Julia Peterkin, DuBose Heyward, and T. S. Stribling as notable among the South's "liberal" writers (Myrdal 468). Faulkner's disappointing and conflicted attitudes over race matters have been well documented, but a contemporary outsider found his fiction far from reactionary.

6   In 1960 Faulkner replied to a request from a former black employee that he pay for a lifetime membership for him in the

NAACP. Faulkner refused him on the ground that the organization had made some recent "mistakes" in not encouraging blacks to be more responsible: "As I see it, your people must earn by being individually responsible to bear it, the freedom and equality they want and should have" (*Selected Letters*, 444). Jehlen quotes this letter in its entirety to illustrate Faulkner's racial paternalism (118–119).

7 Private contracting of prison labor seems to have declined rapidly by the late 1920s, but the public continued to enjoy the benefits of such labor: "the chain gang or some version of the county road camp remained supreme in southern penology into the 1940s and 1950s" (Kirby 217). Grimwood discusses the importance of the chain gang as a metaphor for sharecropping in *The Wild Palms* (123–126).

8 When Faulkner decided that he would like to host a party for the MGM crew filming *Intruder in the Dust* in Oxford in the spring of 1949, he agreed with his wife and aunt that Juano Hernandez, the Puerto Rican playing Lucas Beauchamp, could not be invited to Rowan Oak without including his black hosts in Oxford, too. Such social mixing of the races rarely if ever occurred in the deep South; Faulkner consented to Hernandez's exclusion.

9 Jehlen refers to the "foolishness" of Lucas's moonshining and treasure hunting (Jehlen 122). Weinstein takes them seriously, both symbolically and practically (Weinstein 60–61).

10 Though Willis acknowledges that nature had been spoiled by civilization well before Sam Fathers and the other hunters celebrate their wilderness rituals, she argues that the wilderness contains some "Utopian" content despite its partial contamination with the ways of commerce and its objectionably masculinist exclusiveness (87). Willis's views of the basic opposition between historical regimes of production, between the plantation and the market, between the wilderness and the commissary, and between myth and history rest on well sanctioned methods of Marxist economic analysis. They should, I think, be complemented by an examination of the operation of racist ideology and the capacity of outdated ideological and social forms to reinvent themselves with differences.

WORKS CITED

Blotner, Joseph L. *Faulkner: A Biography*. One-volume edition. New York: Random House, 1984.

Cash, W. J. *The Mind of the South*. New York: Knopf, 1941.

Faulkner, William. *Absalom, Absalom!*. The corrected text. New York: Random House, 1936. Vintage International edition, 1990.

Go Down, Moses. New York: Random House, 1942. Vintage International edition, 1990.

Faulkner in the University: Class Conferences at the University of Virginia 1957–1958. Ed. Frederick L. Gwynn and Joseph L. Blotner. New York: Random House, 1959.

Selected Letters of William Faulkner. Ed. Joseph Blotner. New York: Random House, 1977.

Godden, Richard. *Fictions of Capital: The American Novel from James to Mailer*. Cambridge: Cambridge University Press, 1990.

Grimwood, Michael. *Heart in Conflict: Faulkner's Struggle with Vocation*. Athens, GA: University of Georgia Press, 1987.

Horkheimer, Max and Theodor Adorno. *Dialectic of Enlightenment*. Trans. John Cumming. New York: Continuum, 1987.

Irwin, John T. *Doubling and Incest/Repetition and Revenge: A Speculative Reading of Faulkner*. Baltimore: Johns Hopkins University Press, 1975.

Jehlen, Myra. *Class and Character in Faulkner's South*. New York: Columbia University Press, 1976. Paperback edition, Secaucus, NJ: Citadel Press, 1978.

Kirby, Jack Temple. *Rural Worlds Lost: The American South 1920–1960*. Baton Rouge: Louisiana State University Press, 1987.

Moreland, Richard C. *Faulkner and Modernism: Rereading and Rewriting*. Madison: University of Wisconsin Press, 1990.

Myrdal, Gunnar, with the assistance of Richard Sterner and Arnold Rose. *An American Dilemma: The Negro Problem and Modern Democracy*. New York and London: Harper & Brothers, 1944.

Rowe, John Carlos. "The African-American Voice in Faulkner's *Go Down, Moses*." In J. Gerald Kennedy, ed., *Modern American Short Story Sequences: Composite Fictions and Fictive Communities*. Cambridge: Cambridge University Press, 1995: 76–97.

Silver, James W. *Mississippi: The Closed Society*. New York: Harcourt, Brace and World, 1964.

Snead, James A. *Figures of Division: William Faulkner's Major Novels*. New York: Methuen, 1986.

Southern, David W. *Gunnar Myrdal and Black-White Relations: The Use and Abuse of 'An American Dilemma' 1944–1969*. Baton Rouge: Louisiana State University Press, 1987.

Sundquist, Eric J. *Faulkner: The House Divided.* Baltimore: Johns Hopkins University Press, 1983.

Weinstein, Philip M. *Faulkner's Subject: A Cosmos No One Owns.* New York: Cambridge University Press, 1992.

Willis, Susan. "Aesthetics of the Rural Slum: Contradictions and Dependency in 'The Bear'." *Social Text* 2 (Summer 1979): 82–103.

3

Go Down, Moses and the Discourse of Environmentalism

JUDITH BRYANT WITTENBERG

GO Down, Moses is one of the more remarkable fictions created by William Faulkner in his long and distinguished career. Technically complex, the work's method – the intricate interweaving of previously published short stories with added material designed both to connect the segments and to increase their thematic range – has over the years elicited arguments among critics as to whether it is a collection of short stories, a "composite" (Creighton), or a cohesive novel; recent judgments essentially concur that it is a novel unified by its compelling portrayal of an abusive social and economic system and that its somewhat fragmented method and varied tone echo central thematic elements and intentionally deconstruct the very notion of facile aesthetic closure (Morris 123). The novel depicts a large number of distinctive characters, more perhaps than any other Faulkner novel, many of them connected by blood through several generations of a complicated family that includes individuals of both Caucasian and African heritage. The portrayal of its central figure, Isaac McCaslin, is sufficiently ambiguous that commentators continue to disagree as to the implications of his rhetoric and his behavior (Wall summarizes much of the controversy). The conceptual scope of *Go Down, Moses* is impressive, because its rich and provocative treatment of racial, class, and gender issues is splendidly amplified by its consideration of the interrelationship of the human problems with basic questions concerning not only land ownership – most vividly apparent in Isaac McCaslin's radical gesture of repudiation – but also the very essence of the connections between human beings and the natural environment.

49

Some years after the publication of *Go Down, Moses,* Faulkner spoke on several occasions about the European colonizers' effect on the American landscape over the centuries, sometimes doing so in a general way, sometimes making particular reference to that portion of wilderness exemplified in the Mississippi Delta region often referred to as "The Big Bottom." During a question and answer period at the University of Virginia, Faulkner described the tragedy inherent in the moment of origin when land ownership in the United States essentially began, when it was first taken by white settlers from the indigenous inhabitants, who "held the land communally." There is a "ghost of ravishment that lingers in the land," said Faulkner, "the land is inimical to the white man because of the unjust way in which it was taken from [the Indians]" (*Faulkner in the University,* hereafter FIU:43). In another moment, he lamented the widespread destruction of the wilderness, reflecting that it is "a change that's going on everywhere; man spends more time ruining the wilderness than he does finding something to replace it" (FIU 68). On other occasions, he spoke somewhat more equivocally. Asked, for example, whether "The Bear" portion of the novel was about a conflict between man and the wilderness, Faulkner said that he was not asking anyone to choose sides, that we need rather "to compassionate the good splendid things which change must destroy." He went on to say that process of change in the landscape must be judged by its outcome: "to clear wilderness just to make cotton land, to raise cotton in an agrarian economy of peonage, slavery, is base because it's not as good as the wilderness which it replaces. If the destruction of the wilderness means more education for more people and more food, then it was worth destroying" (FIU 277). Some of Faulkner's willingness to accept certain alterations in the environment may be attributable to his participation in the "ravishment" represented by land ownership and cultivation: At the time he wrote *Go Down, Moses* he was, says his biographer, the largest landholder in Oxford, Mississippi, owning, in addition to the land on which his house Rowan Oak stood, the single largest tract of land inside the town – the twenty-four acre Bailey's Woods – and a three-hundred-and-twenty-acre farm outside Oxford, complete with tenant farmers and even a commissary (Blotner 986–1069). In at least one instance, Faulkner evinced pride in his land acquisitions, telling someone that "I own a larger parcel of it than anybody in town" (*Selected Letters* 128). Nevertheless, in his 1942 novel, as in other fictions such as *The Hamlet* and *Big Woods*, and in his public statements, Faulkner thoughtfully explores the tragic implications of land ownership and the depredation of the wilderness, although he does so in a manner sufficiently ambiguous as to suggest the complexity of the issues.

Because of this, *Go Down, Moses* is often cited as one of the most significant American novels – if not *the* most – that deals with wilderness and environmental themes. Leonard Lutwack describes the work as the "most eloquent statement on behalf of the wilderness" (169), and John Elder calls it one of the works "which most profoundly depicts the shifting balance between man and nature in American history" (44–45). Annette Kolodny says that the portrait of Isaac McCaslin and his ameliorative response to the contemplation of the land which man has "deswamped and denuded and derivered in two generations" should be read not merely as a story of the South but as a comment on the course of an entire nation's pastoral impulse, and that Ike's characterization is Faulkner's attempt to introduce a vocabulary that will do away with the notion of the land as something to be either possessed or preyed upon and to suggest a human-land relationship based on reciprocity and communality (Kolodny 140, 145).

To say that *Go Down, Moses* is a protoecological work of fiction which, in significant ways, anticipates the outpouring of environmental concern that occurred about twenty years later would be, perhaps, to overstate the case. Nor is it primarily focused on what has been called "the biotic community." It is a distinctly anthropocentric novel whose conceptual fulcrum is the complicated interracial dramas that constitute its various segments and whose overarching thematic focus is the destructive long-term impact of the colonizing white settlers on those from whom they took the land – in Northern Mississippi, the Chickasaw and

51

Choctaw Indians – and on those whom they brought to work the land – the slaves forcibly transported from Africa – and their descendants. As depicted in *Go Down, Moses,* the inmixing of these three groups over the generations ironically complicates and amplifies the destructiveness rather than in any way ameliorating it. At least one critic asserts that, for Faulkner, behind these tragic human dramas of the nineteenth and twentieth centuries depicted in the novel lies the shadow of the larger tragedy in which they all originated, the seizing of the land centuries before and its subsequent clearing for cultivation. This, says Leonard Lutwack, is "the original Southern sin," "the guilt of the past," in which all the subsequent social and economic failures dramatized by Faulkner have their source (Lutwack 163; see also Breaden).

Faulkner's compelling depiction in *Go Down, Moses* of various attitudes toward the Mississippi landscape and its function as background for a series of morally problematic and frequently destructive human relationships not only gives the work a breadth and resonance found only in a handful of his greatest fictions, it also connects the novel with a significant aspect of the cultural context, the growing discussion of environmentalism and ecology that was taking place during the 1930s and the 1940s even as Faulkner was completing the various segments of his 1942 novel and undertaking the process of integrating them into a cohesive whole. This discussion, so splendidly articulated in differing ways by major figures of the era like Faulkner and Aldo Leopold, author of the landmark environmental work, *Sand County Almanac,* would intensify in ensuing decades and eventuate in statutory reforms such as the Endangered Species Act of 1973. It might seem less than appropriate to compare Faulkner's great novel, so clearly centered on complex familial and other human interrelationships, to a series of nonfiction works that include nature journals, autobiographies, and hortative essays and almost exclusively focus on environmental issues, but the linkages between them are compelling and important. *Go Down, Moses* and texts by Aldo Leopold and other environmental thinkers of the period not only reveal their authors as grappling conceptually with many of the same ideas, they also evolved from a more general and increasingly well articulated discussion of environmental issues.

* * * * *

The thematic nexus of such works as *Go Down, Moses* and some of the environmental texts – the delicate and crucial interconnection of all things on and of this earth, and the alarming human capacity for violent disruption – makes it productive to approach them via an intertextual reading. In "The Bounded Text," Julia Kristeva speaks of any text as "a permutation of texts, an intertextuality," in which discourses from other texts "intersect" one another (Kristeva 36). This vision of discursive intersection suggests the notion of "network," which, in some sense, is the dominant trope not only of *Go Down, Moses* but of ecological thinking generally, which views the entire earth as a single community that functions as an intricate web. Relevant to this intertextual exploration is SueEllen Campbell's identification, in her discussion of the shared premises of deep ecology and poststructuralism, of "the network" as the most important of the fundamental parallels between the two theoretical positions. Both ecologists and poststructuralists, says Campbell, critique the dominant structures of Western culture such as the idea of an authoritative locus of hierarchical meaning or of the human being as either central or centered, substituting instead the notion of "the network." She notes the presence of this trope in work by Derrida, Lacan, and Foucault, the latter of whom asserted, for example, that any individual is merely a "node within a network" (quoted in Campbell, 207). Similarly, ecologists believe that all elements on earth are interconnected, that any organism is simply a "knot" in the biospherical field. Although Faulkner's 1942 novel is certainly not explicit about this viewpoint, traces of it are evident, and the environmentalist critics speak quite pointedly about the biotic community. Thus, as both thematic focus and critical strategy, the network metaphor is not only appropriate for approaching such texts but for placing their ideas in a conceptual context.

The richness of this context is striking. The works of the

1940s by William Faulkner and the environmentalists had deep historical roots. To say that Faulkner was not the first American writer to use a regional wilderness as both backdrop and "character" in his work is to state the obvious; any student in an American literature survey course quickly notes the extensive role played by "nature" in the literature of the past two centuries. Although the concept of nature itself has been revealed as problematic in recent discussions by Lawrence Buell, Myra Jehlen, and others, who have critiqued it as a hegemonic formation, it has long been acknowledged as a, perhaps the, formative influence in traditional American writing (see Buell). The sense of an unspoiled landscape – the "fresh, green breast of the new world," in Fitzgerald's memorable phrase from *The Great Gatsby* (Fitzgerald 182) – capable of inspiring and restoring the human spirit "corrupted" by civilization has, says Leo Marx, never lost its powerful hold on the American imagination (Marx 3, passim).

For novelists, poets, and essayists from Cooper, Emerson, and Thoreau to Jeffers and Faulkner, the imaginative influence of nature has been of major significance. Their work has, as we know, affected both literary successors and environmental activists; although the relationship of the former to their predecessors may perhaps be marked by subconscious anxiety, that of the latter has frequently been characterized by enthusiastic admiration. Thoreau, for example, whose classic work *Walden* (1854) had a limited impact beyond a small group of literary admirers, became an environmental hero in both the United States and Great Britain in the later twentieth century, inspiring both those who supported ecological activism and those in favor of animal rights. Thoreau was, it has been pointed out, an ecologist before we called it "ecology" (Nash, *Rights* 35–36). It also seems worthy of note that central elements of *Walden* recur, mutatis mutandis, in *Go Down, Moses:* the concepts that in the wilderness one confronts "only the essential facts of life" and is thus able to respond simply and meaningfully; that ownership of property is deleterious, an "imprison[ing]" state; that hunting is a stage of "education" for a youth, one to be outgrown, superseded by the recognition that he is profoundly connected to his fellow creatures; and the presence of the ledgers whose objective records of expenditures function in counterpoint with Thoreau's philosophical ruminations.

More geographically relevant to Faulkner's work, if less significant in a literary sense, are the "pen pictures" of the vanishing Mississippi wilderness of the 1840s published at the beginning of the twentieth century in a Tupelo newspaper by W. F. Clayton. Seeming to anticipate aspects of *Go Down, Moses* with their description of the "vast forests" of the past as they were when inhabited only by Indians, teeming with wild game and "covered with great upstretching trees" (13–14), Clayton's sketches lament the way in which, by the beginning of the twentieth century, the landscape had been adversely affected by loggers and planters, who destroyed "nature's handiwork," felling the great trees for lumber and replacing them with fields of corn and cotton. In passages that sound almost like source material for portions of "Fire and the Hearth," Clayton also assails the distractions of a capitalist economy that occupies men with pecuniary gain and expresses sentimental affection for figures of the past such as the "old black mammy" whom children of white households often regarded as "almost a savior" (Clayton 22, 27).

Writers such as these were part of the ongoing literary celebration of the vanishing wilderness and its salutary challenges to those individuals who encountered it in its pristine state. Their voices also contributed to a more general discussion about environmental issues that grew in strength in the United States during the 1930s and 1940s. The environmental crisis was not new, however, and some have suggested that it had its roots in early Judeo-Christian thought, originating in God's reported command to mankind to "be fruitful, and multiply, and replenish the earth, and subdue it: and have dominion over the fish of the sea, and over the fowl of the air, and over every living thing that moveth upon the earth" (Genesis 1:28; see White). In the United States, the myth of the West as a "vacant continent" awaiting the "civilizing" impact of European settlers encouraged development in a westerly direction in a process championed most vociferously in Congress by Thomas Hart Benton and celebrated in literary works like Whitman's "O Pioneers," which, says Henry Nash Smith, "gave final imaginative expression to the theme of manifest destiny" (Smith 47–48). This process accelerated after the Civil War with the manipulations of land speculators and the efforts of the railroad builders, whose new form of transportation delivered eager settlers into the "empty" landscape at a rapid pace. Nevertheless, awareness of the problems created by such incursions, formerly confined to an enlightened few, increased as a result of the cataclysm of World War I, which revealed that an increasingly industrialized and urbanized world had also become prey to international power struggles, thus raising further doubts about the effects of so-called "civilization" on human beings and the natural environment (Nash, *Wilderness* 160).

Although the environmental crisis in the United States was deep-rooted and increasing with each decade, the public perception that it was fast assuming disastrous proportions grew during the 1930s and 1940s as a result of some consciousness-raising events and the publication or rediscovery of several influential texts. One such event was the terrible "dust bowl" phenomenon of the 1930s, when thousands of farmers were dispossessed from the plains region as a consequence of both an extended drought and their destructive land-use methods of previous years. Those ultimately responsible were the "sodbusters" of an earlier era, who had tilled the soil with wanton disregard for the impact of their techniques; the dust bowl expulsions of the 1930s, pervasively tragic in human terms, might also be seen as the revenge of the land. As Donald Worster notes, the farmers' attitude toward the environment – their disregard for the land as a permanent home and their heedless depletion of the soil – ironically resulted in their own poverty and dislocation (Worster 226). The incremental effects of such human behavior were analyzed in an influential work of the mid-1930s, Paul Sears's *Deserts on the March*, which criticized prevailing land-use practices like those that eventuated in the dust bowl. Such occurrences contributed to the increasing awareness that the commodity approach of an earlier conservation figure like Gifford Pinchot was based on concern for the nation's economy rather than nature's and that it had negative implications for the environment. The gradual tipping of the conceptual scales from nature-as-commodity to nature-as-community was an important development in the environmental thinking of this era, and vestiges of both viewpoints can be seen in *Go Down, Moses.*

* * * * *

The impact of significant environmental events such as the dust bowl was augmented by the publication or rediscovery of some crucial texts in the field, which both increased the public awareness of the basic issues and brought the discussion forward in meaningful ways. Max Horkheimer and Theodor Adorno, in their *Dialectic of Enlightenment* (1944), argued that, since the eighteenth century, Western thought had confronted two contradictory stances: the first, a dedication to the search for intrinsic value and ultimate purpose – "the mythic imagination," or "the mythological," in which reason is devoted to transcendence – and, the second, a desacralized view of the world that makes reason instrumental in the drive for the domination of nature – "enlightenment." In this dialectic, individuals believe either in human subjection to nature or nature's subjection to the self (Horkheimer and Adorno 32, and passim; see also Worster); one can see the operation of a comparable dialectic in *Go Down, Moses,* particularly in the commissary discussion between Ike and his cousin Cass. Cass asserts the value of their ancestor's efforts that overcame nature, that "cleared" the "wilderness of wild beasts and wilder man" and "translated it into something to bequeath to his children," whereas Ike refutes him with statements grounded in a more sacral view of nature and a sense that the relationship of human beings to the land must be one of mutuality and community (245–246). Faulkner critics have often faulted Ike for his reliance on such "weak" arguments; indeed, the rationalist "man over nature" thought characterized by Horkheimer and Adorno as "enlightenment" has often informed critical assessments of *Go Down, Moses* (Wall 153). In the environmental writing of this period, however, one sees a certain trend toward the side of the dialectic termed by Horkheimer and Adorno "the mythological," as some influential texts began to question the ascendancy of the human over the natural world. Works which appeared – or re-appeared – during the 1930s and 1940s and to varying degrees had an effect on the public discussion, included George Perkins Marsh's *Man and Nature,* Albert Schweitzer's *My Life and Thought: An Autobiography,* John Muir's journals, and Aldo Leopold's *Sand County Almanac.*

Marsh's *Man and Nature,* first published in 1864, was rediscovered in the 1930s, in large measure because of the growing evidence during that era that the "hostile influence of man" on the environment of which Marsh had warned his readers seventy years before was now coming to some sort of destructive fruition. Marsh raised the "great question," later explored by Horkheimer and Adorno, as to "whether man is of nature or above her" and anticipated the ecological perspective of the twentieth century with his concern about the hazards of human interference "with the spontaneous arrangements of the organic or the inorganic world" (Marsh 3, 36, 186–187, 465). One of Marsh's dedicated readers was John Muir, founder of the Sierra Club; Muir's journals, published in 1938, evinced a reverential view of nature very much like "the mythological" as later defined by Horkheimer and Adorno. Muir described Yosemite Valley as a "temple," a place of "divine beauty," where "God's glory is . . . written upon every field and sky" (Muir 39, 47). Like the Mississippians W. F. Clayton and William Faulkner, whose devout regard for the majestic southern wilderness of earlier years informed their work, Muir also described the forests of the American South in awed terms, as a place of "noble trees," many of them as tall as one hundred feet (Muir 365). Albert Schweitzer, known more for his humanitarian efforts than for his ecological ideas, revealed in his 1933 autobiography, *My Life and Thought,* a concern for an ethics grounded in "Reverence for Life," asserting that a human being can be ethical "only when life, as such, is sacred to him, that of plants and animals as much as that of his fellow man" (Schweitzer 185, 188).

All these individuals and their texts contributed to the growing discourse on environmental issues, but Aldo Leopold is in many ways the pivotal figure of the period, despite the fact that he and his work were little known to the wider public until after his death. Not only is Leopold's posthumously published *Sand County Almanac* regarded by many as the "bible of the ecology movement" of the latter twentieth century, but in his own intellectual development Leopold also mirrors the changes occurring during the 1930s and 1940s. At the start of his career in forestry, Leopold was a utilitarian in the Gifford Pinchot mold and dedicated to the extermination of predatory animals. He was, however, profoundly influenced by two events and evolved into the figure we know today, an environmental ethicist of the first order. The first of these events was a meeting in 1931 with Charles Elton, author of the 1927 landmark work *Animal Ecology,* which posited the notion of the food chain and the close linkages between the plant and animal "communities." Elton noted the interdependence of all of earth's inhabitants and asserted that when human beings attempt to exploit nature's resources, they disturb its balance (Elton 9, 16, 52–54). It has been suggested that discussions with Elton during this meeting essentially "converted" Leopold to a more ecological view of nature (Worster 300); his founding of the Wilderness Society in 1935 revealed his dedication to the preservation of areas where natural communities could continue without further human disruption. A second event that visibly contributed to the evolution of Leopold's thinking about the environment was his 1936 camping trip in the Sierra Madre region of Mexico, when he experienced what might be called an epiphany, dramatically responding to the realization that this area of Mexico represented the wilderness at its most pristine and that the wild areas of the United States had already been adversely affected by human efforts.

In subsequent years, he began the process of preparing the volume known as *Sand County Almanac,* which may be productively read against *Go Down, Moses.* Although Leopold's work is undramatized nonfiction prose and Faulkner's is a complex and ambiguous narrative, the two texts have important conceptual parallels and carry on a fruitful intertextual dialogue. Somewhat comparable in their methods, the two texts are also parallel in their consideration of certain basic environmental themes. Their techniques – the weaving together of interconnected fragments – are appropriate for their topic, the complicated linkages between the discrete but interrelated members of the earthly community. *Sand County Almanac* has an unusual three-segment structure, each portion of which is composed of smaller pieces: The first part is a series of short prose poems and anecdotes, seasonally arranged for continuity; the second, a group of topical essays inspired by a variety of geographical locales; and the third, several long and issue-oriented essays that elucidate points of ecological doctrine and rise to hortatory eloquence. The seven-part structure of *Go Down, Moses* comprises distinct narratives connected by genealogical ties among their principal characters, recurrent thematic elements, and a chronological movement generally forward in time. Despite a degree of unity and some sense of "progression," if you will, in each text, there is an equally strong counter-pull away from the center; this methodological tension is clearly suitable to the subject, a community paradoxically at once interconnected and atomized.

Faulkner's and Leopold's texts are most closely affiliated in the comparability of their central concepts. In his 1948 foreword, Leopold identifies himself as one of that minority which sees "a law of diminishing returns of progress" (Leopold xvii) – a group to which Faulkner, with his increasingly explicit criticisms of everything from radios to government regulations, obviously also belongs – and makes his central point, that human beings are capable of abusing the land "because we regard it as a commodity belonging to us." He writes that when we instead "see land as a community to which we belong, we may begin to use it with love and respect. There is no other way for land to survive" (Leopold xviii–xix). Throughout the book, Leopold assails the "profit-motive," "economic self-interest," and the view of land as a commodity, proposing instead an ethic based in the "community concept." Some of these ideas had been put forth in somewhat different terms but with equal fervor a hundred years before by Karl Marx, who assailed the notion of private property, seeing land ownership as originating in "robbery" and inevitably involving exploitation of other human beings as well as of the land itself. In his early writings, Marx asserted the close interdependency of human beings and nature and proposed, in place of land ownership, something he called "association," which would restore the intimate relationship between man and the land (Marx 116).

Echoes of both Leopold and Marx can be found in Faulkner's portrayal of Isaac McCaslin, who repudiates the large land holdings that he inherits, becoming one "who owned no property and never desired to since the earth was no man's but all men's" (4). The portrait of Ike stands in dramatic apposition to that of his cousin Cass, whose view is that land can not only be owned, but should be developed and cultivated, in order to make it "worthy of bequeathment," a "legacy and monument" (245). That the adumbration of Ike's viewpoint frames the text of *Go Down, Moses* and recurs in many of the segments obviously accords it greater conceptual weight than that of the property owner Cass. Ike even provides his own exegesis of the passage from Genesis that has troubled ecologists, asserting that God "created man to be His overseer on the earth and to hold suzerainty over the earth and the animals on it in His name, not to hold for himself and his descendants inviolable title forever, . . . but to hold the earth mutual and intact in the communal anonymity of brotherhood" (246). Moreover, in assailing the plantation economy toward which land-use was directed in the South – an "edifice intricate and complex and founded upon injustice and erected by ruthless rapacity and carried on even yet with at times downright savagery not only to the human beings but the valuable animals too" (285) – Ike provides an implicit critique of capitalism itself.

* * * * *

In many of its other portrayals, *Go Down, Moses* offers either direct or subtle evidence of a skeptical view of a commodified approach either to land or to the methods of production. In the fictive northern region of Mississippi, the "original sin" was committed by the Chickasaw Indian Ikkemotubbe. As well as proving himself capable of murder and the appalling sale of his own family into slavery, Ikemotubbe also, in profound violation of Indian belief, sells some of his people's land. The confluence of complicity in murder, slavery, and land conveyance in the brief portrait of Ikkemotubbe is, however exaggerated, telling. As Faulkner himself said some years after the publication of *Go*

61

Down, Moses, the acceptance by white settlers of property signed over to them by indigenous peoples unleashed a "ghost of ravishment that lingers in the land" (FIU 43).

As the 1942 novel makes clear, this ravishment has tainted all those who participated in it, however indirectly. Even Lucas Beauchamp, consigned to the economic margins by his part-African ancestry, appears in "Fire and the Hearth" as a greedy would-be landowner who regards the field he cultivates as "his own" and believes he "would own the land if his just rights were only known," if Cass had not "beat him out of his patrimony" (36); Lucas accordingly regards Ike as "apostate to his name and lineage" for "weakly relinquishing the land which was rightfully his" (39). Lucas is also a striving entrepreneur whose musings on the threats to his illegal but profitable manufacture of alcohol by a new "competitor" turn him into a comical caricature of capitalist obsession. He is anxious about the "interruption of business" and "loss of revenue" created by the need to move his still and fears the incursion into "his established trade, his old regular clientele," longing for the recent days in which he held a virtual monopoly on the local trade (33–36). Lucas's preoccupation with his economic ambitions makes him heedless toward the landscape, even the Indian mound, which he is prepared to desecrate in his quest for gold. The prospect of digging it up "did not bother him" (42). One of the more memorable aspects of *Go Down, Moses* is the portrait of Lucas Beauchamp, who is, like Ike McCaslin, a figure at once sympathetic and problematic.

Although Lucas himself has been profoundly and adversely affected by the white colonizers' attitudes toward property – both land and, under slavery, human beings – he appears to have internalized them and to have unwittingly accepted other attitudes with which they are closely linked. These are evident not only in his obsession with material gain, but also in his patriarchal assumption that male lineage is superior, his nostalgia for the days in which he believed that "men . . . were men," and his possessive attitude toward the women in his family, whom he often treats as if they were objects of exchange. A product of slavery, Lucas has become himself enslaved to the sort of thinking that initially made it conceivable. In this instance, Faulkner's critique is subtle and rather humorous. More pointed and earnest is Leopold's invocation of "god-like Odysseus" as an example of ethical blindness when he hangs a dozen slave girls whom he suspected of misbehavior. Even an heroic figure such as Odysseus, says Leopold, proves capable of egregious behavior when it involves "disposal of property." Leopold then asserts that ethical treatment must be extended not only to all human beings but to the environment itself; this is his "land ethic." He calls for a repudiation of the notion of "land [as] the slave and servant" and its replacement with the idea of "land the collective organism" (Leopold 237, 261). Leopold's vivid example of the extension of destructive attitudes toward property into the human sphere and his subsequent plea for a much more communo-ethical stance toward land and human beings are reflected in Faulkner's character portrayals. In *Go Down, Moses,* the region and its peoples all seem to have been contaminated to a greater or lesser degree by the concepts that flow from the notion that land can be dominated and possessed. Belief in the ownership of land is part of what Marc Baldwin describes as a "culture of domination" and is causally linked to claims to the ownership of blacks and women (Baldwin 200).

In addition to questioning the very concept of land ownership, *Go Down, Moses,* like *Sand County Almanac,* places high value on wilderness; indeed, the word itself is the most frequently used uncommon term in the novel, recurring fifty times in the second half (Capps). Wilderness is valuable not only in and of itself but also for the sort of enriching experiences it offers to responsive human beings. Faulkner's novel is, among other things, a bildungsroman in which the natural environment plays a crucial role in the development of the central character. For Ike McCaslin, the wilderness has both educational and spiritual significance; it is "his college," the place where he "entered his novitiate," as if "witnessing his own birth" (202, 187). The moment in which Ike discards the items which are the last vestiges and "taints" of "civilization" and "relinquishe[s]" to the wilderness is the one in which he fully discovers the profundity of his connection to his natural surroundings and is rewarded by the sight, first, of a fresh paw print and, next, of the bear itself, "as big as he had expected, bigger, dimensionless against the dappled obscurity" (200). Leopold also discusses the way in which a woodland can provide an individual with a "liberal education," referring to the "many lessons" he himself learned there (Leopold 77); again, observing two youths canoeing, he reflects on the educational merits of wilderness travel, which allows one the "complete freedom to make mistakes" and teaches the "rewards and penalties for wise and foolish acts" (Leopold 120).

For Faulkner's Ike, as well as for Leopold, hunting proves to be a crucial element in this "education." Although it might seem paradoxical that those with a reverence for nature and its creatures would be willing to kill any of them – and Thoreau certainly saw hunting as a questionable "phase" of moral development, a phase which must be outgrown by any "humane being" – it is the case that many of the environmentalists, even those most fervent about conserving wild areas, saw hunting as integral to the wilderness experience. Leopold, say his editors, considered hunting as "important to the building of character" (Brown and Carmony 67), and he wrote an essay (1925) entitled "A Plea for Wilderness Hunting Grounds." In it, he argued for hunters' access to wilderness areas and discussed the merits of the pursuit. Faulkner, too, spoke in more or less positive terms about hunting, also with reference to its function as a symbol of the "pursuit" which he described as fundamental to human life – "the pursuit is the thing, not the reward, not the gain"; and he asserted that one should "slay the animals with the nearest approach you can to dignity and decency" (FIU 272, 54). Pursuit is a central motif in *Go Down, Moses,* from the comical, if unnerving, chase of Tomey's Turl in "Was," where the slave is treated as if he were an animal quarry, through the various wilderness segments, to the quest by Mollie Beauchamp, in the final portion of the novel, to retrieve the body of her grandson. Ike's accession to manhood is clearly signified by his brave and sometimes solitary tracking of the old bear; though he does not participate in this culminating kill, his shooting of a deer and his willing involvement in the pursuit and final confrontation with Old Ben indicate the range and strength of his courage. As a youth, Ike feels "alien" to the woods "until he had drawn honorably blood worthy of being drawn," and the tutelary figure Sam Fathers tells him that, once he has killed a deer, "You'll be a hunter. You'll be a man" (169–170). When he succeeds and is ritualistically marked with the hot blood of the felled deer, Ike becomes "one with the wilderness which had accepted him" and "ceased to be a child and became a hunter and a man" (171).

Still, as both Faulkner and some of the environmental writers made clear, in some memorable moments, a hunter's awed response to a game animal he has been avidly pursuing precludes the possibility of killing it. John Muir records an instance when he was part of a group hunting the wild sheep of Shasta, whose leader was a huge ram, "a noble old fellow." During the pursuit the ram stopped for a moment, "his form and noble horns . . . clearly outlined against the sky." Muir experiences guilt, feeling wolflike in his "savage exhilaration" at the hunt, and another member of the party simply gazes at the ram until he disappears into a thicket (Muir 199–200). Similarly, in *Go Down, Moses*, when Sam Fathers, who equates hunting with manhood, sees an impressive buck "full and wild and unafraid," walking "tremendous" and "unhurried," he simply salutes him, saying, "Oleh, Chief. Grandfather" (177). In thus paying awed tribute to the majesty of one manifestation of nature's grandeur, Sam reveals that such moments of reverence for the splendor of a single wild animal can overcome the will to slay of even a dedicated hunter.

Intriguingly, in both *Sand County Almanac* and *Go Down, Moses*, the most compelling symbol of the wilderness that is at once magnificent, threatening, and threatened is an immense and fearsome, yet ultimately vulnerable, bear. Much of Leopold's work reveals his special reverence for the grizzly bears that once inhabited portions of the American West in substantial numbers. In a 1936 article on "Threatened Species," Leopold warned that all conservation projects in or near locations inhabited by grizzlies must be judged "in the light of whether they help or hinder the perpetuation of the noblest of American mammals" (Brown and Carmony 195), and in *Sand County Almanac*, he memorializes a single specimen, the huge bear known as Old Bigfoot. This bear lived on the Arizona mountain called Escudilla, from which he descended each spring to kill and feast on one of a local rancher's cows; the force of Old Bigfoot's murderous assault was such that in one recorded instance the dead cow looked as if "she had collided with a fast freight [train]." Old Bigfoot's predatory habits, along with his size, made evident by his "incredible tracks," and his elusiveness – "no one ever saw the old bear" – imbue him with an extraordinary mystique; all those living in the area are frightened of and fascinated by him. Although he "claimed for his own only a cow a year, and a few square miles of useless rocks," nonetheless "his personality pervaded the [surrounding] county" (Leopold 142–143). With bleak and sarcastic brevity, Leopold records the arrival in the area around Escudilla of a government trapper looking to exterminate "destructive animals," who finally, after several vain attempts, manages to slay Old Bigfoot only by ambushing him with a set-gun in a defile. "The last grizzly walked into the string and shot himself" (144). Fearsome in life yet pathetically reduced by the nature of his death and the patchy pelt he leaves behind, Old Bigfoot becomes an emblem not only of the ultimately pointless assaults on predatory animals but also of the very wilderness itself, venerable and splendid yet vulnerable to destruction by ill conceived human efforts.

Faulkner's Old Ben, who occupies a similar emblematic position in *Go Down, Moses,* evinces many of the same characteristics as Old Bigfoot; he is simultaneously menacing and awe-inspiring, a creature known to and feared by all who venture into the region he inhabits. The moment in which Ike McCaslin first sees Old Ben has quasi-religious overtones – the bear appears almost as if by magic in a sunlit glade – and recalls, says Susan Donaldson, Mircea Eliade's definition of the mystical encounter with the sacred (Donaldson 39). Like Old Bigfoot, the bear is terrifying to human beings as a result of his size, his elusiveness, and his predatory habits; he is even compared to a locomotive, that darkly ambiguous emblem of human incursion and "progress." The moment in which Old Ben "breaks the rules" established by his human admirers, who have hitherto pursued him regularly but without fully murderous intent, and kills one of Major de Spain's colts, proves to be the moment in which his doom is sealed. Although Old Ben's animal antagonist, the yellow-eyed and fierce dog Lion, is in many ways a more worthy opponent than Leopold's government trapper, Faulkner's bear is also compromised at the moment of death, brought down in a wild encounter with the less-than-admirable Boon Hogganbeck. Symbolically, the bear "crashed down . . . as a tree falls" (231).

Fittingly for its genre, Faulkner's narrative of the death of the majestic bear is enriched by several memorable human characterizations; thus, although, as in Leopold's text, the demise of a single animal signifies the loss of something splendid and unreplaceable, as well as the ultimate decay of the surrounding wilderness, it also resonates throughout the rest of that segment of the novel and beyond. The impact on the part-Chickasaw Sam Fathers is devastating; not long after Old Ben dies, Sam follows him, having fallen insensate to the ground in the very moment the bear is fatally stricken. Ike knows instinctively "that Sam too was going to die" (236). In both Leopold's and Faulkner's texts the death of an awe-inspiring creature at the hands of unworthy human beings heralds the decline of the wild areas he inhabits.

* * * * *

Even as the Leopold and Faulkner texts evince reverential regard for the wilderness and its enriching effects on those who respect it and respond to it, they serve finally as elegiac witnesses to the ways in which it is being destructively altered, moving gradually and perhaps irrevocably beyond the point of reclamation. In the penultimate essay of *Sand County Almanac,* Leopold says that wilderness is, for the philosophical observer, "something to be loved and cherished," the more so because "many of the diverse wildernesses out of which we have hammered America are already gone" (Leopold 265). He appraises the "value of wilderness" in humanistic terms, asserting that in its "raw" form it "gives definition and meaning to the human enterprise" (Leopold 279). In this same passage, Leopold also comments on the "humility" required to see the fundamental worth of the wilderness.

Although Leopold here refers to intellectual humility, of which he believes "only the scholar" is capable, the response he describes is something akin to the emotions experienced by Faulkner's young Ike McCaslin. In revising the material from which he created *Go Down, Moses,* Faulkner was careful to amplify the reverential aspect of the boy's attitude toward the wilderness (Creighton 122). As Ike confronts the big woods and their quality, "profound, sentient, gigantic and brooding," he feels "dwarfed" (169). Ike experiences "an abjectness, a sense of his own fragility and impotence against the timeless woods, yet without doubt or dread" (192). During his last trip into the Big Bottom as a youth, Ike is shocked at the sight of the changes wrought by further development of the area, responding with "grieved amazement" to the changes in the "doomed wilderness" (303, 306). The train now looks like a "snake" bearing with it into the landscape "the shadow and portent of the new [planing] mill" (306). This segment – which follows the all-important passages in which Ike expresses his deeply held belief that the land he has relinquished was "never mine to repudiate" (246) and makes his horrifying discovery of the human "crimes" recorded in the family ledgers – ends with further haunting images of decline: a visit to the graves of Lion and Sam Fathers, Boon's demented hammering of his dismembered gun, and Ike's saluting of the enormous rattlesnake, "ancient and accursed," evocative "of pariah-hood and of death" (314).

In the penultimate segment of *Go Down, Moses,* "Delta Autumn," which is also the bleakest portion of the novel, the darkness of the human story has its parallels in the depredations visited upon the landscape. Now the aged Ike sees himself and the wilderness "as coevals," the "two spans running out together" (337), connected in such fundamental ways that the decay of the wilderness mirrors his. He reflects sadly on how dramatically it has diminished, retreated, been beaten back by loggers, planters, developers, and automobiles until only a small portion of the splendid vastness remains. It has been "deswamped and denuded and derivered in two generations" (347). Ike, too, is in decline, descending into the last moments of old age and impending death. Worse, physical decay is imaged in ethical inadequacy; Ike McCaslin displays in these passages a haunting failure of moral imagination and a revelation of racist attitudes, as he tries desperately to buy off the part-black grand-daughter of Tennie's Jim, who has come looking for Roth Edmonds, and tells her to marry a man of her own race. He also pointlessly offers her, for her son, the hunting horn that once belonged to General Compson. It is as if the "ruined woods" have visited their "retribution" even on an individual who has always evinced only profound respect and admiration for them. The tale ends with a telling description of Ike lying alone and corpselike, barely protected from "the constant and grieving rain" (347–348). The hunt, too, has been degraded, in the formerly taboo killing of a doe.

The final section of *Go Down, Moses,* although not directly concerned with the environmental issues so central to other portions of the novel, nevertheless focuses on some of the indirect and unfortunate consequences of the original mistreatment of the land – the fatal deracination of a member of the youngest generation of Beauchamps, who has been expelled from the land by an Edmonds and executed in a northern prison for killing a policeman, and, in the ultimate manifestation of the racial divide, the complete failure of one well-meaning white person, Gavin Stevens, to comprehend the powerful grief of the elderly black woman he is trying to help. The downward emotional trajectory of Faulkner's novel conforms to its moving portrayal of a complicated and ultimately tragic array of interracial and intergenerational relationships and its evocation of a vanishing natural splendor that has been destroyed by the same attitudes that, extended into the human sphere, result in misunderstanding and exploitive treatment. Like Aldo Leopold's landmark work *Sand County Almanac,* which a Secretary of the Interior called "a noble elegy for the American earth" (quoted in Sessions 34), *Go Down, Moses* explores with elegiac eloquence essential questions about the interconnections between human beings and their environment. That these two texts, which represent in differing ways culminating moments in their own genres and in the emerging discourse of environmentalism of an earlier era, continue to engage a wide public with their memorable descriptions of the natural world and with their provocative considerations of ethical questions, bears plangent witness to their timeless significance.

WORKS CITED

Baldwin, Marc D. "Faulkner's Cartographic Method." *Faulkner Journal* 7:1–2 (1991–92), 193–214.

Blotner, Joseph. *Faulkner: A Biography.* New York: Random House, 1974.

Breaden, Dale G. "William Faulkner and the Land." *American Quarterly* 10:3 (Fall 1958), 344–357.

Brown, David E. and Neil B. Carmony, eds. *Aldo Leopold's Wilderness.* Harrisburg, PA: Stackpole, 1990.

Buell, Lawrence. "American Pastoral Ideology Reappraised." *American Literary History* 1:1 (Spring 1989), 1–29.

Campbell, SueEllen. "The Land and Language of Desire: Where Deep Ecology and Post-Structuralism Meet." *Western American Literature* 24:3 (Fall 1989), 199–211.

Capps, Jack L., ed. *Go Down, Moses: A Concordance to the Novel.* Ann Arbor: University Microfilms, 1977.

Clayton, W. L. *Olden Times Revisited,* ed Minrose Gwin. Jackson: University Press of Mississippi, 1982.

Creighton, Joanne V. *William Faulkner's Craft of Revision.* Detroit: Wayne State University Press, 1977.

Donaldson, Susan. "Isaac McCaslin and the Possibilities of Vision." *Southern Review* 22:1 (Winter 1986), 37–50.

Elder, John. *Imagining the Earth: Poetry and the Vision of Nature.* Champaign: University of Illinois Press, 1985.

Elton, Charles. *Animal Ecology.* London: Sidgwick & Jackson, 1927.

Faulkner, William. *Go Down, Moses.* New York: Vintage, 1990.

Faulkner in the University, eds. Frederick Gwynn and Joseph Blotner. Charlottesville: University Press of Virginia, 1959.

Selected Letters of William Faulkner, ed. Joseph Blotner. New York: Random House, 1977.

Fitzgerald, F. Scott. *The Great Gatsby.* New York: Scribner, 1953.

Horkheimer, Max, and Theodor Adorno. *Dialectic of Enlightenment.* Trans. John Cumming. New York: Continuum, 1987.

Kolodny, Annette. *The Lay of the Land.* Chapel Hill: University of North Carolina Press, 1975.

Kristeva, Julia. "The Bounded Text," in *Desire in Language,* ed. Leon Roudiez. New York: Columbia University Press, 1980, pp. 36–63.

Leopold, Aldo. *A Sand County Almanac.* New York: Ballantine, 1966.

Lutwack, Leonard. *The Role of Place in Literature.* Syracuse: Syracuse University Press, 1984.

Marsh, George Perkins. *Man and Nature* [1864]. Cambridge, MA: Belknap Press of Harvard, 1965.

Marx, Karl. *Early Writings.* Trans. and ed. T. B. Bottomore. New York: McGraw-Hill, 1964.

Marx, Leo. *The Machine in the Garden.* New York: Oxford University Press, 1964.

Morris, Wesley and Barbara. *Reading Faulkner.* Madison: University of Wisconsin Press, 1989.

Muir, John. *John of the Mountains: The Unpublished Journals of John Muir,* ed. Linnie Marsh Wolfe. Boston: Houghton Mifflin, 1938.

Nash, Roderick. *The Rights of Nature.* Madison: University of Wisconsin Press, 1989.

Wilderness and the American Mind, rev. ed. New Haven: Yale University Press, 1973.

Schweitzer, Albert. *My Life and Thought: An Autobiography.* Trans. C. T. Campion. London: George Allen & Unwin, 1933.

Sears, Paul B. *Deserts on the March* [1935]. 3d. ed., rev. Norman: University of Oklahoma Press, 1959.

Sessions, George. "Ecological Consciousness and Paradigm Change." In *Deep Ecology,* ed. Michael Tobias. San Marcos, CA: Avant Books, 1988.

Smith, Henry Nash. *The Virgin Land.* New York: Vintage, 1950.

Wall, Carey. "*Go Down, Moses:* The Collective Action of Redress." *Faulkner Journal* 7:1–2 (1991–92), 151–174.

White, Lynn, Jr. "The Historical Roots of Our Ecologic Crisis." *Science* 10 (March 1967), 1203–1207.

Worster, Donald. *Nature's Economy: A History of Ecological Ideas.* New York: Cambridge University Press, 1985.

4

Her Shape, His Hand: The Spaces of African American Women in *Go Down, Moses*

MINROSE GWIN

IN *Playing in the Dark: Whiteness and the Literary Imagination,* Toni Morrison has argued that Africanism is essential to the definition of Americanness and American modernity, as well as to the major themes and presumptions of the white North American literary imagination. In particular, she believes that the white literary imagination has been the ideological site of "the manipulation of the Africanist narrative (that is, the story of a black person, the experience of being bound and/or rejected) as a means of meditation – both safe and risky – on one's own humanity" (Morrison, *Playing* 53). Morrison calls for literary and cultural inquiries into "[h]ow the representation and appropriation of that narrative provides opportunities to contemplate limitation, suffering, rebellion, and to speculate on fate and destiny" in white North American literature. Criticism of this kind, she believes, "will show how that narrative is used in the construction of a history and a context for whites by positing history-lessness and context-lessness for blacks" (Morrison, *Playing* 53).

In part, at least, such literary criticism is no stranger to Faulkner studies in general, and to *Go Down, Moses* in particular. Thadious M. Davis, in *Faulkner's "Negro": Art and the Southern Context,* has explored the workings and reflections of racial stereotype in Faulkner and the symbolic valence of "Negro" for the southern writer who wishes to convey concepts such as "slavery, sexuality, primitivism, fraternity, endurance, hope," and historical contexts such as the antebellum South, metaphors for change, or social issues and problems (T. M. Davis 26–27). Lee Jenkins, whose *Faulkner and Black-White Relations* takes a psychoanalytic approach to race in Faulkner's fiction, bases his analysis on the premise that, in the minds of whites (Jenkins seems to mean white men), "the black" (he seems to mean black men) has become the mythic personification of repressed impulses and desires of whites, "the embodiment of the very idea of contamination and of the idea that the mind is divided against itself" (Jenkins 58–60). Eric Sundquist, on the other hand, explores Faulkner's "turbulent search for fictional forms in which to contain and express the ambivalent feelings and projected passions that were his as an author and as an American in the South" (Sundquist x).[1]

Morrison's suggested areas of inquiry, however, are more focused on narrative than symbol.[2] Like Henry Louis Gates, she problematizes "race" as an unceasing and dynamic cultural narrative whose telling and retelling have historically served Eurocentric interests.[3] She asks how the Africanist story in literature by white Americans becomes "the specter of enslavement, the anodyne to individualism" that makes freedom seem free (Morrison, *Playing* 56) and how Africanist character in such literature "is used to limn out and enforce the invention and implications of whiteness" (Morrison, *Playing* 52). In my reading of *Go Down, Moses,* certainly a novel with what Morrison would call an "Africanist presence at its center," I should like to complicate these questions to ask how Africanist *female* narrative and character function in a text written by a white southern male in large part about their exploitation as Africans and as women.[4] I am hoping to excavate what Chandra Mohanty has called a complex *"relationality"* (her emphasis) – relations of power "not reducible to binary oppositions or oppressor/oppressed relations." Mohanty believes that feminist analysis must focus on the interactions between "the idea of multiple, fluid structures of domination which intersect to locate women differently at particular historical conjunctures" and at the same time "the dynamic oppositional agency of individuals and collectives and their engagement in 'daily life' " (Mohanty 13). Although Mohanty is discussing relations of power in social and political life for Third-World women, her focus on these intersections of the cultural spaces of domination and the cultural spaces of resistance resonates with certain questions I want to pose about *Go Down, Moses* and its ideological productions and reflections.

I am primarily interested in the relations between material, cultural, and narrative space as they are occupied by African American women in the novel. This is not to imply that I see these three kinds of spaces as distinct or noncontiguous. By material space I mean representations of actual physical structures, landscapes, geographies, to which cultural space with its permutations of the dynamic and incessant workings of ideology is intimately linked; as is narrative space, constructed through the productions of language and what Faulkner might call not-language, or silence. In terms of *Go Down, Moses*, I am wondering how the cultural space of African women in North America – circumscribed by race and sexual vulnerability and described by African American women in their own critical and literary productions – may (or may not) translate to narrative space in a literary text written by a white southern man at least in part *about their predicament.* And what do the material spaces – the actual physical sites – that black female characters occupy in these texts indicate about where their Africanist narratives are located, both in terms of their agency as African women and the valence their stories and presence carry? In short, where are their stories *located* in *Go Down, Moses?* And what do they mean?[5]

I am wondering also whether Faulkner is participating in what Morrison has called the objectification of "bound blackness" even as he describes the white patriarchal usage of black women, or whether their narrative space – their boundedness within the stories of old Carothers McCaslin's abuse of Eunice and his own daughter Tomasina and their resulting deaths, Zack Edmonds' appropriation of Molly Worsham (later spelled "Mollie"), Roth Edmonds' abandonment of his unnamed lover, cousin, and mother of his son – take up more space than we might at first think. Do their stories push at the boundaries created by the white male characters whose narrative spaces exceed theirs and whose stories may appear to confine theirs to the space of objectification? In exceeding the narrative spaces created for them as objects of oppression, do their stories radicalize Faulkner's text in ways we have not yet recognized? Or, do they (their Africanist stories, their bounded yet somehow excessive spaces) serve a master narrative which has historically unfolded, as Morrison has maintained, "in the rhetoric of dread and desire" and whose manipulation of Africanness has offered "historical, political, and literary discourse a safe route into meditations on morality and ethics; a way of examining the mind-body dichotomy; a way of thinking about justice; a way of contemplating the modern world" (Morrison, *Playing* 64)? Or . . . are these questions whose answers are not mutually exclusive?

Textual and Cultural Spaces

To situate these questions, we may turn to anthropological studies of the relations of space and ideology. Feminist studies in architecture and planning, as well as anthropology, have shown how space and its allocations in the material world "reflect and reinforce the nature of gender, race, and class relations in society" (Weisman 1). In a study of the gendering of space among the Marakwet of Kenya, anthropologist Henrietta Moore argues that material space – for example, a village – can be read as a text. To understand space as a text, Moore says, is "to conceive of the spatial order as something more than merely the physical manifestation, or product, of activities conducted in space. Spatial texts may, therefore, be said to have both a history and a future" (Moore 81). My project here is to try to read a white male literary text as both producing and reflecting African American female space. The kind of reading I am undertaking relies on a corporeal imagination, on a sense of how physical bodies inhabit physical space and how the lived experience of the female body, in this case the black female body, converges with representational practice, in this case the representational practices displayed and enacted in *Go Down, Moses.*

Following Terry Eagleton and Fredric Jameson, Moore suggests that a text, be it a book or a living space, is not *representative* of ideology but is a *product* and *producer of* ideology, "of the 'lived' conditions of social reality. . . . For ideology is not expressed, reflected or reproduced in the text; rather, it produces and is produced by the text, transforming it into a particular and irreducible representation" (Moore 87–88). In short, spatial texts (of Marakwet's gendered living arrangements) – and, I would argue, textual spaces (for example, of *Go Down, Moses*) – reveal the dynamic and incessant productions of ideology, as do our readings of them.[6] The relation between ideology and the text is therefore one of continually "produced representation" (87). Because spatial representations "express in their own logic the power relations between different groups, they are therefore active instruments in the production and reproduction of the social order" (Moore 89). An analysis of spatial representations in a narrative about such power relations may lead to a more grounded notion of how those relations are produced, and how literary and cultural productions are inevitably entwined and synergetic.

Go Down, Moses lends itself to a spatial analysis. Obviously, there are distinct narrative divisions into various but interconnected stories. Moreover, one of Faulkner's primary concerns in the novel is space: the receding space of the wilderness, the effects of the (mis)appropriation of space. One of the more haunting images of the novel is that of the young bear that becomes entrapped in a tiny tree after he climbs up to escape the sound of the logging train. He has run out of space; there is no place for him to go. There is a sense throughout the novel of encroaching claustrophobia, of too much being crowded into spaces not meant to hold so much. The town and logging interests encroach on the wilderness, squirrels crowd hysterically in the big gum tree awaiting Boon Hogganbeck's shots, the old ledgers in the old store are too small a space to contain, in all their cultural and historical implications, the outrageousness of old Carothers McCaslin's crimes and the tragic stories of Eunice and Tomasina, whose lives are squeezed into cryptic phrases in the ledger book, a book whose original purpose was to record profit and loss.

In a very literal way, the constriction of these women's lives into the spaces of the ledger produced by white men is contiguous with the cultural spaces that African American women have historically occupied in a white dominated culture. In *Black Feminist Thought,* Patricia Hill Collins discusses how "white male power is largely predicated on Black female subordination" (Collins 189) and how that subordination has been figured in placing the black female body in the space of the object of display. The treatment of black women's bodies in nineteenth-century Europe and the United States, Collins argues, may well have been "the foundation upon which contemporary pornography as the representation of women's objectification, domination, and control is based" (Collins, 168). The exhibition in Europe of African women such as Sarah Bartmann, the so-called Hottentot Venus, reveals "the importance of gender in maintaining notions of racial purity" and demonstrates "that notions of gender, race, and sexuality were linked in overarching structures of political domination and economic exploitation" (Collins 169). As Sander L. Gilman points out, there were other African women displayed throughout early nineteenth-century Europe. In an 1850 erotic engraving, for example, a white man sitting in an easy chair with his dog at his feet is gazing through an uptilted telescope at the buttocks of an African woman who is standing on top of a large rock bent over with her skirts hoisted. (The man's dog is also gazing upward.)[7] In a cultural analysis, these kinds of displays may be seen as physical manifestations of the historical paradox of African American women's material space, especially within southern slavery. Though women were often not so confined physically as men, their material spaces were nevertheless extremely confining and hazardous. The "open" space of the slave ship decks or the master's house made African women highly visible targets for what Angela Davis has called "an institutionalized pattern of rape" (A. Davis 23). For them, "open" space within white culture was not open but highly claustrophobic and dangerous.

Harriet Jacobs, for example, writes in *Incidents in the Life of a Slave Girl,* that she preferred the nine-by-seven-by-three-foot (at its highest point) garret in which she lived for seven years to the more constricted and treacherous "open" space she occupied as a female slave in the house of a master intent on raping her:

To this hole I was conveyed as soon as I entered the house. The air was stifling: the darkness total. A bed had been spred [sic] on the floor. I could sleep quite comfortably on one side; but the slope was so sudden that I could not turn on the other without hitting the roof. The rats and mice ran over my bed. . . . This continued darkness was oppressive. It seemed horrible to sit or lie in a cramped position day after day, without one gleam of light. Yet I would have chosen this, rather than my lot as a slave. (Jacobs, 114)

The solitary confinement and severe hardship of closed physical space may have been preferable to the terrors of "open" space in which, as Collins says, the black woman was "viewed as an object to be manipulated and controlled" (Collins 69).

It is not surprising to find that space is an issue of great importance in African American women's fiction. In Morrison's *Beloved,* when Paul D is protesting Sethe's hospitality to Beloved, a young black woman who appears out of nowhere, Sethe replies heatedly, "feel how it feels to be a coloredwoman roaming the roads with anything God made liable to jump on you. Feel that" (Morrison, *Beloved* 68). In the end, Beloved herself, who has had feelings of breaking into pieces, is dispersed into open space. She is everywhere and nowhere: "Down by the stream in back of 124 her footprints come and go, come and go. They are so familiar. Should a child, an adult place his feet in them, they will fit. Take them out and they disappear again as though nobody ever walked there" (Morrison, *Beloved* 275). In Octavia Butler's *Kindred,* Dana, a black woman living in a Los Angeles suburb in the 1970s, finds herself moving across time to enter the space of nineteenth-century slavery on a Maryland plantation. In what becomes a more and more difficult and injurious journey, Dana extends herself across the spaces of geography, history, and race to save her white male forebear, an oppressive slave master, and keep him alive so that he can coerce another black woman, Dana's great-great-grandmother, to have sexual relations with him, thereby beginning the family into which Dana would eventually be born. Dana finds herself caught up in the confinement of her great-great-grandmother's impossible position. The seeming openness of the space of time travel becomes increasingly restricting and dangerous as Dana gets caught, literally, in the vise between past and present and, in the end, escapes only by losing part of her body.

The fact that open spaces historically have been closed (objectifying, confining, dangerous) for African American women in a society dominated by white men situates any spatial analysis of the narrative configurations of *Go Down, Moses* on slippery footing. If "open" is "closed," culturally and often materially, then how are we to measure black women's narrative space – the space of the Africanist/womanist story (if it exists) – in a white man's text where, if literary and cultural representations are correlative, the opening up of narrative space for black female characters may actually be their closing down? If we believe with Moore, however, that spatial texts/textual spaces are both products and producers of ideology, *as are their readings,* it may be important to explore just how ideology is translated spatially in narrative, not just in terms of *Go Down, Moses* and Faulkner but within a more general inquiry into the relations between cultural and literary productions.

For example, *Go Down, Moses* begins with the inscription:

TO MAMMY
CAROLINE BARR
Mississippi
[1840–1940]
Who was born in slavery and who
gave to my family a fidelity without
stint or calculation of recompense
and to my childhood an immeasur-
able devotion and love

The space of this epigraph may be seen as open. It pays homage to Caroline Barr and becomes the foyer leading into the novel. On the other hand, it summons the closed equation: black mammy equals love (devotion, fidelity), the figure of "mammy" and the ideological construction of mammy equals love being based materially, as Trudier Harris has pointed out, on the black mammy's separation from her own home space and family "in order to rear generation after generation of whites who would, ironically, grow up to oppress Blacks still further" (Harris 36).[8]

80

Centered on the page, the inscription to Caroline Barr is circumscribed by white space up, down, and on either side. It has the look of an epitaph on a gravestone.

Just as the epigraph page may be pictured spatially as the foyer which opens into the larger narrative space of *Go Down, Moses*, the novel's ending, or closure, is Gavin Stevens' commentary on Mollie (earlier spelled "Molly") Beauchamp's desire to bring her criminal grandson home for a decent burial and her instructions to the newspaper editor that he print all there is to know about "Butch" Beauchamp's death (which, as she may or may not know, was by execution). Although Mollie cannot read, she wants to "look at hit" in the newspaper. Stevens' thoughts about her request close the story and the book:

Yes, he thought. *It doesn't matter to her now. Since it had to be and she couldn't stop it, and now that it's all over and done and finished, she doesn't care how he died. She just wanted him home, but she wanted him to come home right. She wanted that casket and those flowers and the hearse and she wanted to ride through town behind it in a car.* "Come on," he said. "Let's get back to town. I haven't seen my desk in two days." (365)

These thoughts by the white man whose paternalism has prevented him from understanding or participating in Mollie Beauchamp's grief encloses her and her articulations of what she sees as her grandson's betrayal by Roth Edmonds and, by implication, her people's betrayal at the hands of whites. Stevens misreads Mollie's text and closes down the space of her Africanist narrative articulated in her chants: "Roth Edmonds sold my Benjamin. . . . Sold him to Pharaoh and now he dead" (62). Although Faulkner uses the device of a white man's misunderstanding the stories of black characters (for example, the sheriff's deputy telling the story of Rider's grief, which he mistakes for its lack, in "Pantaloon in Black"), Stevens' statements, if meant ironically or not, may seem an odd way of ending this particular story and this particular novel. Stevens mutes Mollie's narrative of accusation and mourning by trivializing her grief. The final enclosure of Mollie within the space of his paternalism is similar to the enclosure of Caroline Barr's life in the equation of mammy equals love that begins the novel. There is no reopening of black women's spaces, or recognition of the problematics of the position of white manhood vis-à-vis southern history such as that which informs Quentin Compson's last agonizing exclamation about the South in *Absalom, Absalom!: "I don't hate it! I don't hate it!"* (*AA* 303) The cultural implications of Mollie Beauchamp's accusations, and of the novel as a whole, seem to become muffled rather than intensified by Gavin Stevens' final pronouncements, which, in the end, distance us from her voice.

Between these two perimeters, the mammy bounded in a whitespace of "love," "fidelity," "devotion," and the mammy's grief and reproach enclosed by white paternalism (Mollie is described as the only mother Roth Edmonds ever knew who nurtured both his body and spirit [113]), *Go Down, Moses* fluctuates throughout, both opening up and closing down black women's narrative space. And those spaces that contain the stories of black women are not always what they seem. Sometimes these women leave us wondering – as we do in "Pantaloon in Black" when Rider sees the ghost of his dead wife Mannie appear and then dissolve – whether they were ever there at all.

The Space of the Watching Woman

"The Fire and the Hearth" opens with Lucas Beauchamp moving his still because George Wilkins, his daughter Nat's lover, has set up another still on Roth Edmonds' land. Lucas has reported George's activities to Roth and is afraid that his own still, which has been operating for twenty years without Roth's knowledge, will be found in a search for George's. In the process of moving and burying his still in the middle of the night, he finds a coin which he believes is part of a buried treasure. As day breaks and he rises to his feet to go home, he hears a crash and then the sounds of "the quarry fleeing like a deer across the field and into the still night-bound woods beyond" (40). He finds the prints of his daughter's feet where she had squatted in the mud and spied on him. At first this space of the watcher gives Nat a certain amount of power in dealing with her father, her lover, and the law. Although Nat is clever and defiant in her dealings with both Lucas and George, in the end she does not get what she wants: a back porch and a well to make George's house more livable for her. In the last conversation of the story, Lucas and George are making plans to set up the new still George has bought with the money Lucas gave him for the porch and well. Patriarchal power closes around Nat when she is not watching, and the space she has demanded for herself is withdrawn by father and husband.

I want to trace Nat's footsteps, as Lucas does when he sees "the print of his daughter's naked feet where she had squatted in the mud, knowing that print as he would have known those of his mare or his dog, standing over it for a while and looking down at it but no longer seeing it at all" (41), yet this is impossible. Nat makes her prints in this story, but dissolves in the end in man talk carried on by African American men. She watches, but her watching and her clever manipulations dissolve like footprints being washed away. At the end of the story, Lucas, who had earlier been intent on teaching George a lesson *"about whose daughter to fool with next time"* (61) transfers possession of Nat to George, thereby transforming Nat's enclosure from "daughter" to "wife." When George asks how they are going to tell Nat she won't be getting a back porch or a well, Lucas replies: "I don't give no man advice about his wife" (75). Like Gavin Stevens' dismissal of Mollie's grief in "Go Down, Moses," "The Fire and the Hearth" ends with an enclosure of black female space. Nat the watcher, the clever daughter, is made into a wife. It is interesting that Faulkner, in a humorous way, propels two black men, Lucas and George, into the space of patriarchal power, ironically giving them ideological kinship to Old Carothers McCaslin.

Another woman described as watching is Tennie Beauchamp. In "The Bear," Ike recalls from his childhood, his mother Sophonsiba surprised her brother Hubert Beauchamp with his mulatta mistress, who is wearing Sophonsiba's dress, and ran her out of the house screaming, "My mother's house! Defiled! Defiled!" (289). In the midst of the uproar, Ike remembers

(. . . Tennie's inscrutable face at the broken shutterless window of the bare room which had once been the parlor when they watched, hurrying down the lane at a stumbling trot, the routed compounded of his uncle's uxory: the back, the nameless face which he had seen only for a moment, the once-hooped dress ballooning and flapping below a man's overcoat, the worn heavy carpetbag jouncing and banging against her knee, routed and in retreat true enough and in the empty lane solitary young-looking and forlorn yet withal still exciting and evocative and wearing still the silken banner captured inside the very citadel of respectability, and unforgettable.) (289–290)

From the margins, Tennie watches the white family eject the unnamed mulatta mistress from the crumbling house and send her scrambling down the road. Here black women occupy both the spaces of the watcher and the one being watched, subject and object, inside and outside. The space of this recollection within "The Bear" carries a peculiar tension and resonance, for, like Clytie Sutpen in *Absalom, Absalom!* whose tragic face gazing from the window of Sutpen's Hundred becomes the avatar of the inevitable consequences of white greed and rapacity, Tennie's "inscrutable face" both frames the historical moment and becomes the space on which that moment is written. An impersonal syntax ("the routed compounded of his uncle's uxory") records an image of the rapidly retreating back of one African American woman and the unreadable text of another's face.

What is the space between these two women, one still and unreadable – like Clytie, framed by the window of a crumbling big house – the other whose face we cannot see hurrying down the lane and off the page? *What lost stories were here?* What "safe spaces," black women's locations "for resisting objectification as the Other," as Collins would call them (Collins 95), have been lost? Tennie's "inscrutable face" remains inscrutable. And the mulatta mistress remains a blank spot in the novel, a rapidly receding figure whose story remains untold.

The Space of the Ledger

It is this untold story that haunts Patricia Williams. Specifically, the erasure of her great-great-grandmother's life and narrative provides the original vehicle for Williams' *The Alchemy of Race and Rights,* a brilliant study of the relations of race to individual and social contractual rights in this country. A lawyer and professor of law, Williams describes the bill of sale for her great-great-grandmother as "a very simple document but lawyerly document, describing her as 'one female' and revealing her age as eleven." In a county census record of two years later, "on a list of one Austin Miller's personal assets she appears again, as 'slave, female' – thirteen years now with an eight-month infant" (Williams 17). Since coming into possession of these documents which testify to her great-great-grandmother's existence and its circumstances, Williams writes that she has tried "to piece together what it must have been like to be my great-great-grandmother," a girl purchased by a thirty-five-year-old Tennessee lawyer known to be temperamental and wealthy, after a fight with his mother about prolonged bachelorhood:

> I imagine trying to please, with the yearning of adolescence, a man who truly did not know I was human, whose entire belief system resolutely defined me as animal, chattel, talking cow. I wonder what it would have been like to have his child, pale-faced but also animal, before I turned thirteen. I try to envision being casually threatened with sale from time to time, teeth and buttocks bared to interested visitors. (Williams 18)

Like Ike McCaslin and his cousin McCaslin Edmonds, Williams searches historical texts (letters and legal opinions written by her great-great-grandfather) for clues to the past. She yearns to find "the shape described by her [great-great-grandmother's] absence in all this" (Williams 19). She sees "her shape and his hand" – "the habit of his power and the absence of her choice" – in the ideologies of power and dominance that continue to shape legal codes and cultural practice in the United States (Williams 19).

In "The Bear," the space of the ledger is the repository of the overlapping spaces of southern white male rapacity and the need of white men for contemplation and exorcism. For Ike the ledger is inhabited by ghosts of southern history:[9]

> a lightless and gutted and empty land where women crouched with the huddled children behind locked doors and men armed in sheets and masks rode the silent roads and the bodies of white and black both, victims not so much of hate as of desperation and despair, swung from lonely limbs. (278)

The space of the commissary – the place of commerce for the white men who owned it and the land – encloses the shelf of ledgers, the desk and "the corner where it sat beside the scuffed patch on the floor where two decades of heavy shoes had stood while the white man at the desk added and multiplied and subtracted" (279). Within these concentric material spaces – the store, the desk, the ledgers – the female slave is enclosed as the signifier of "bound blackness." For Ike and his cousin McCaslin, who, like Quentin and Shreve in *Absalom, Absalom!*, are constructing their own narratives of family and history, the small yet large, closed yet open, narrative spaces occupied by Eunice and Tomasina reveal what Morrison has called "the not-free," that is, the "conveniently bound and violently silenced black bodies" which perform "duties of exorcism and reification and mirroring" for the white imagination (38–39). That the ledger is the space for performing those duties for Ike is abundantly clear:

> To Him it was as though the ledgers in their scarred cracked leather bindings were being lifted down one by one in their fading sequence and spread open on the desk or perhaps upon some apocryphal Bench or even Altar or perhaps before the Throne itself for a last perusal and contemplation and refreshment of the Allknowledgeable before the yellowed pages and the brown thin ink in which was recorded the injustice and a little at least of its amelioration and restitution faded back forever into the anonymous communal original dust. (250)

As in Williams' documents, the text that can be read is written in white men's hands. The sections on Eunice and Tomasina are written by Ike's father Theophilus ("Uncle Buck") and his uncle Amodeus ("Uncle Buddy"), who both read and recorded the text of sexual violence perpetrated by their father; Buck and Buddy's text is read and its exorcistic function reproduced by Ike and McCaslin; *their* stories, of course, are of Faulkner's doing. In all these white men's "hands," the black woman is a shape that is both revealed and obscured.

In a sense, then, the bodies of Eunice the mother and Tomasina the daughter occupy a double space of exchange: Their bodies are used sexually (and for their reproductive value as well) in the material spaces of their lives as slaves; those bodies, as objects of contemplation (Morrison might say, "on demand and on display") within the space of the ledger, are manipulated again by Ike and McCaslin in performing their "duties of exorcism and reification and mirroring." Because those duties are grounded in the same principles of exchange that rely on the objectification of bound blackness, they lack the recuperative power to generate new ideologies of empowerment. They are as meaningless as Uncle Buck and Uncle Buddy's move into the slave quarters. Ike can only condemn "that whole edifice intricate and complex and founded upon injustice and erected by ruthless rapacity and carried on even yet with at times downright savagery" (285); he is unable to construct new ideological foundations in place of the edifice he decries because he is unable to read black women's texts outside the space of the ledger, the space of bound blackness.

Throughout his life, Ike's inability to envision the Africanist female narrative apart from the space of the white man's ledger sets the tenor of his relations with black women within the material and cultural spaces of the postbellum South they and he inhabit. His two important encounters with African American women reveal his inability to see them as subjects outside the space of bound blackness. Both encounters involve the trespass of material space. In "The Bear" we are told how Ike tracks down Fonsiba, who is Tennie and Terrel (Tomey's Turl) Beauchamp's daughter, to give her one thousand dollars from her grandfather Carothers McCaslin's estate. Having failed in a similar mission to find Tennie's Jim the previous year, he is driven by guilt through "slow interminable empty muddy December miles crawled and crawled," telling himself, "*I will have to find her. I will have to. We have already lost one of them. I will have to find her this time*" (265). When he does find her, in a log cabin in the midst of a "roadless and even pathless waste of unfenced fallow and wilderness jungle," he sees not a woman in her kitchen but

crouched into the wall's angle behind a crude table, the coffee-colored face which he had known all his life but knew no more, the body which had been born within a hundred yards of the room that he was born in and in which some of his own blood ran but which was now completely inheritor of generation after generation to whom an unannounced white man on a horse was a white man's hired Patroller wearing a pistol sometimes and a blacksnake whip always. (265–266)

What Ike sees is not Fonsiba but bound blackness, and his relationship as a white southern man (the Patroller?) to bound blackness. When he later asks her if she is all right, she answers, "I'm free" (268), to which he does not respond but simply goes to the bank and arranges for the money to be paid to her at three dollars a month for the next twenty-eight years. In this scene, which is introduced as he and McCaslin read the ledger within the store, Ike trespasses on Fonsiba's space but does not recognize that he does so. He sees only that she and her husband are living in poverty, and he mistakes that physical poverty for spiritual poverty. For him, Fonsiba is only a body, "only the tremendous fathomless ink-colored eyes in the narrow, thin, too thin coffee-colored face watching him without alarm, without recognition, without hope" (268).

Reflections of Ike's blindness within his bounded whitespace, Fonsiba's watching eyes, like Nat's and Tennie's, give a fleeting glimpse of an opening into African woman's narrative space. There is another story here, another space opening with Fonsiba's assertion, "I'm free" (268). Ike, and Faulkner, rapidly retreat from that story. After Fonsiba utters those two words, which would seem to be but the beginning of her Africanist narrative, the next sentence in the text is a description of the town near Fonsiba and her husband's cabin; the bank; the bank's president, who is given more of a story than Fonsiba herself ("a translated Mississippian who had been one of Forrest's men too" [268]); and Ike's financial arrangements for Fonsiba. Upon hearing those words, "I'm free," Ike rapidly retreats from Fonsiba's material space which he has trespassed upon. He re-enters the space of the ledger, the world of commerce in which debts of all kinds can be paid in money, the space owned by white men ("one of Forrest's men too") whose hands inscribe the valuations of the ledger. *That* space is what Ike cannot retreat from, though he tries, for he himself has become its ideological producer and production.

88

And so in "Delta Autumn," when Ike's mulatto kinswoman who is Roth Edmonds' mistress trespasses on the white male space of the hunting tent in the woods, with a baby in her arms, Ike, an old man, can only fumble with the envelope of money and thrust it at her, again aware of her watching eyes, "or not the eyes so much as the look, the regard fixed now on his face with that immersed contemplation, that bottomless and intent candor, of a child" (341). Like Clytie, calling out Rosa Coldfield's name on the stairs of Sutpen's Hundred, the woman says, " 'You're Uncle Isaac,' " to which he replies, " 'Yes . . . But never mind that. Here. Take it. He said to tell you No' " (341).

It is interesting that Ike's first response to the woman indicates disapproval of her sexual behavior outside marriage (as a white woman). He says:

"You sound like you have been to college even. You sound almost like a Northerner even, not like the draggle-tail women of these Delta peckerwoods. Yet you meet a man on the street one afternoon just because a box of groceries happened to fall out of a boat. And a month later you go off with him and live with him until he got a child on you; and then, by your own statement, you sat there while he took his hat and said goodbye and walked out." (343)

The cultural spaces of enclosure – her legal blackness, her and Roth's incest and miscegenation – begin to encircle their exchange as the young woman tells Ike that James (Tennie's Jim) Beauchamp, old Carother's and Tomasina's grandson, is her grandfather. She is Carother's and Tomasina's great-great-granddaughter. The "dark and tragic and foreknowing eyes" (of Tennie, of Fonsiba, of this woman) – the body of bound blackness – materialize suddenly for Ike, and he cries out, "in a voice of amazement, pity, and outrage: 'You're a nigger!' " (344). His response is to cast her out of his space, male space:

"Then go," he said. Then he cried again in that thin not loud and grieving voice: "Get out of here! I can do nothing for you! Cant nobody do nothing for you!" (344)

In a moment that recalls Clytie and Rosa's electrifying "flesh on flesh" connection on the stairs, he touches her hand – "The gnarled, bloodless, bonelight bone-dry old man's fingers touching for a second the smooth young flesh where the strong old blood ran after its long lost journey back to home" – and then draws his hand back beneath the blanket (345). Ironically, then, Ike's space becomes the bounded text. He creates and maintains its boundedness, despite the woman's trespass into male territory marked by man talk and male activity, in which he has been an active participant. There is an interesting hint here of the limitations, exclusions, and potential for the misuse of power within such a space, in contrast to its valorization in the hunting segments of "The Bear," even for morally conscientious men such as Ike.

Moving from "his hand" to "her shape," though, I want to think about the "Delta Autumn" woman's narrative space. As Diane Roberts points out, the woman "imperils both the essential binaries of race and gender" by "passing" as white and as a man (85). Roberts believes that, although she colludes with "the Tragic Mulatta narrative," she is "one of the most articulate female characters in all of Faulkner's fiction" (Roberts, *Faulkner* 86, 88). Despite her brave trespass into white man's space, it seems to me that the woman (I grow weary of calling her this) speaks from within a closed system of exchange, not so much because she is legally black (Roth does not seem to know this), but because, as a devalued woman (Ike's tone makes that much clear), she is entrapped by a masculinist social order. As Luce Irigaray argues, this is "an economy of desire – of exchange – [that is] man's business" (Irigaray 188). The circulation of women among men establishes the operations of patriarchal society; as Irigaray points out, such a social order results in the "trans-formation of women's bodies into use values and exchange values [that] inaugurates the symbolic order" (Irigaray 184, 189). Irigaray suggests that these valuations of women can be categorized into three areas: virgin (pure exchange value), mother (reproductive value), prostitute (use value). The woman's value for Roth obviously falls in the last category; although she loves him and is the mother of his child, he views her as a prostitute.

For the feminist reader, the "Delta Autumn" woman may

reflect and reproduce in troubling ways the ideological components of her own victimization. The woman's profession of love for Roth Edmonds, her willingness to accept the "no" that Ike delivers as Roth's message, her acceptance of Roth's "code" (whatever that is), even her fondness for taking care of his clothes – all speak to a willingness to accept the terms, the bounded spaces, of her own commodification. If, then, she speaks for Eunice and Tomasina, she evokes only their victimization, not their courage, not Eunice's resistance. Ike, in the end, sees her and her baby as the embodiment of his family's crimes and the crimes of southern history. She remains within that bounded space: the story of being "a doe," of being willing to be "a doe." Thus, although Faulkner empowers her to enter male space, he also confines her within a narrative of heterosexual desire within a patriarchal economy that commodifies women and manipulates that desire. She trespasses in order to make her desire known, but, like the hunting horn Ike gives her in lieu of any real help or understanding, it has a hollow sound.

The Space(s) of Molly/Mollie

In "The Fire and the Hearth," when Roth Edmonds looks up from the ledger one day, he sees an old woman walking up the road. He does not recognize her. Not until she comes into the store does he realize she is "the only mother he ever knew," the woman who suckled him and took care of him until he went off to school at age twelve. He fails to recognize Molly Beauchamp because, for the past few years, he has never seen her outside of her own material space. In her own house and yard, where Roth visits her monthly with tobacco and "soft cheap candy which she loved," she is described as moving slowly and painfully with her washing, or sitting on the porch, "her shrunken face collapsed about the reed stem of a clay pipe" (96). She is even more "placed" by several descriptions of her devotion to Roth, her "care for his physical body and for his spirit too . . . who had given him, the motherless, without stint or expectation of reward that constant and abiding devotion and love which existed nowhere else in this world for him" (114). In terms of her space within the novel, Molly(ie), perhaps more than any other character, travels the borders of race and gender. I want to suggest that she is a liminal figure whose identity(ies) as the "Molly" of "The Fire and the Hearth" and the "Mollie" in "Go Down, Moses" together transgress certain expectations of blackness and femaleness that Faulkner simultaneously reflects and deflects. I see Molly's transgression of the spaces of the novel as hinging not so much on her stereotypical role as "mammy," with all its paradoxical implications for both the collapsing of racial barriers and the sustenance of white patriarchal power, but rather on her impact as a character whose liminal narrative can and does *move* across space and time. As a result of her own movement within and *outside of* the male narrative of *Go Down, Moses*, Molly/Mollie has the effect of creating an alternative narrative space, a space which contains both female and Africanist stories.

At the same time, as I've indicated earlier, the openness of such a space may be illusory. Certainly, Molly is not entirely outside of the mammy paradigm, and, in some ways, her character may well be conflated into the closed equation of mammy equals love. As Roberts notes, "*Go Down, Moses* contains places where the Mammy is refigured, only to slip back, in other places, into the inexorable racial and historical context that circumscribes her" (Roberts, *Faulkner* 53). In "The Fire and the Hearth," even when Molly's place within her husband's or Zack Edmonds' house is being contended by the two men, she brings the white baby (Roth) back home with her upon returning to Lucas ("I couldn't leave him! You know I couldn't! I had to bring him!" [49]). This devotion to the white child is questionable for a black woman who has been forced into her situation with Zack, whatever that situation may have been. Yet Molly's energy here, as later in the final story, seems directed toward taking her, and us, out of the male-dominated spaces of the story.

What I find compelling about Molly/Mollie Beauchamp is the *motion* of her character, its/her movement across the landscape of *Go Down, Moses*. When Lucas will not give up the divining machine, Molly takes to the road to get a divorce. And when

Roth Edmonds at first refuses to help her get a divorce and orders Lucas to return the machine and Lucas refuses to do so, Molly takes to the road again: This time she heads for the woods with the divining machine and is found face down in the mud by the creek. She makes her point. When Edmonds takes her and Lucas into Jefferson to the county courthouse to get the divorce and Lucas agrees, under threat of divorce, to give up the machine, she has won the battle. She has contested Lucas's insistence that he be "the man in the house" (117) and has asserted a different, female-centered narrative in its place. Her determined movement within both material and narrative space, despite her infantilization in certain scenes (at the end of the courthouse scene, Lucas gives her a bag of nickel candy and tells her to "gum it" [125]), lend to her actions and person a dignity and resonance that are unmistakably powerful and that make it difficult to dismiss her as a stereotypical mammy.

The Mollie Beauchamp of "Go Down, Moses" leaves home again, this time to come into town and demand that Gavin Stevens find her grandson, who, she is certain, is in trouble. Although she is again described as very small and old, with a shrunken face "beneath a white headcloth and a black straw hat which would have fitted a child," Mollie will not be deterred from her mission. Nor will she be shut up. She tells Gavin her mission, and then begins her chant, which resonates throughout the story: "Roth Edmonds sold my Benjamin. Sold him in Egypt. Pharaoh got him – " (353). After Gavin interrupts her to ask some obvious questions, she begins again:

"It was Roth Edmonds sold him," she said. "Sold him in Egypt. I dont know whar he is. I just knows Pharaoh got him. And you the Law. I wants to find my boy." (353–354)

When Stevens enters the black and white space of the Worshams' household, he finds Mollie and her brother sitting by the hearth and chanting.

"Sold my Benjamin," she said. "Sold him in Egypt."
"Sold him in Egypt," Worsham said.

"Roth Edmonds sold my Benjamin."

"Sold him to Pharaoh."

"Sold him to Pharaoh and now he dead." (362)

The Africanist narrative told from within the space of the call and refrain, as well as the historical and cultural accusations with which the Africanist narrative is laden, sets up a claustrophobic space for Gavin Stevens. He almost runs out of the room and down the hall, thinking, *"Soon I will be outside . . . Then there will be air, space, breath"* (362).

Mollie's Africanist narrative is a counterpoint to and interrogator of the white paternalism that propels Stevens' thoughts and actions. When Stevens collects money to bring home the "dead nigger," he tells "merchant and clerk, proprietor and employee, doctor dentist lawyer and barber" – clearly all white men – that it is for Miss Worsham (not Mollie) that the money is needed. When Beauchamp's body is brought into Jefferson, the hearse circles "the Confederate monument and the courthouse while the merchants and clerks and barbers and professional men" watch from various points around the square. The corpse of a black man is thus encircled by white paternalism and its ideological structures, which, as Mollie believes, probably caused his trouble in the first place. Her insistence that the editor put the story, all of it, in the newspaper is part of her insistence on the Africanist narrative. Though Butch Beauchamp's story is, in many ways, like the story of Beloved, "not a story to pass on" (Morrison, *Beloved,* 275), it is also a story that must be told over and over, as Mollie Beauchamp insists on doing.

Despite Gavin Stevens' perhaps deliberate misreading of that story at the end of the novel, the presence of Molly/Mollie Beauchamp still travels the spaces of *Go Down, Moses.* Her Africanist/womanist narrative seeps out onto the pages, from cover to cover, like a visible watermark across an open book. Whatever else this book is about must be traced through its presence, her shape.

His Hand, Her Shape

And yet. Is it possible that Mollie's utterance of the terrible story of bound blackness actually creates, for the white reader, a space for exorcism – "a safe route into meditations on morality and ethics" – and with it, an attendant sense of the same relief that Gavin Stevens feels in returning to the open/free space of his whiteness as he and the editor watch the hearse carrying Butch Beauchamp's body gather speed and move out of town, "the light and unrained summer dust spurting from beneath the fleeing wheels" (364). After Stevens muses to himself about what I believe he misconstrues as Mollie's desire for a nice funeral for her grandson, he says to the editor, "Come on. . . . Let's get back to town. I haven't seen my desk in two days" (365). Just so do I, the white reader, put down this novel. My question here must be: Do I escape into a freedom made more free by my entry into the "safe" spaces of a novel about African American bondage? Or do I emerge from those spaces with a less safely settled white imagination? Does that novel show the fraudulence of Stevens' return to his desk? Does *Go Down, Moses* place white paternalism into the position of the object on display, and make black women the watchers, the ones whose gaze is accusatory?

I leave these questions unanswered not so much because I do not know the answers (which I admit I do not) but because I believe, with Morrison and in the spirit of her criticism, that these are questions we should be continually negotiating as North American readers of North American literature. I hope that this spatial reading has shown where black women's stories are located and how they are set into motion in *Go Down, Moses*. More problematic is the question of what those stories mean, or I should say what those stories *can* mean. If the relation between ideology and text is one of produced representation, then that production is also enormously complicated by the reader's relation to it. That relation, of reader to Faulknerian text, is in turn compounded in Faulkner studies specifically and American literature generally by having been mediated historically by white men. What I do know and what I have said before is that Faulkner's texts always move beyond what we can say about them.[10] They always embody incommensurability and uncertainty. That embodiment of what we do *not* know is, in the case of *Go Down, Moses*, at least partially situated in the narrative spaces of the African American woman. "Her" shape is not only configured by "his" hand, as was the case with Patricia Williams' great-great-grandmother, but it is also *created* by his hand, the hand of a white southern man whose racist statements, like his sexism, are a matter of record.[11] What are we to make of this?

Morrison believes that (white) Americans have chosen "to talk about themselves through and within a sometimes allegorical, sometimes metaphorical, but *always choked* representation of an Africanist presence" (my emphasis) (Morrison, *Playing* 17). In *Go Down, Moses*, however, Faulkner seems to open and close the spaces of literary utterance for black women, and sometimes to do so simultaneously. The text's engagement with race and gender within the narrative space of African American women both performs and transgresses the material and cultural spaces of region and country, and their attendant ideological permutations. But I do not want to leave this essay on the usual laudatory note of Faulkner's stunning (and it is stunning) ability to keep this kind of textual engagement alive.

Instead I am thinking about how black women in *Go Down, Moses* slip in and out of the spaces of this text, and in such fleeting ways. I am still wondering what Tennie Beauchamp was thinking when she watched Hubert Beauchamp's unnamed mistress get sent packing down the road. I would like to learn what young Molly Beauchamp held in her mind when she was nursing those two babies, and whether Tomasina ever knew why her mother drowned herself. I want to know whether Nat ever got her porch and well. I want to know the "Delta Autumn" woman's name.[12]

NOTES

1 For a more complete list of criticism through 1984 about Faulkner's fictional treatment of racial issues and black characters, see my *Black and White Women of the Old South: The Peculiar Sisterhood in*

American Literature, 190–191, n.5. All three studies point to *Go Down, Moses* as a paradigmatic text in Faulkner's treatment of race, Jenkins viewing the novel as a culmination of Faulkner's thematic concerns (Jenkins 244); Davis, as "a denouement" bringing together a lifetime of thoughts and observations (T. M. Davis 244); Sundquist, as a suffocating "crossing and recrossing of plots and symbolic action" (Sundquist 132). In addition, James A. Snead's *Figures of Division* shows how writing and telling in *Go Down, Moses* re-create and reinforce certain "oppressive social rhetorics" – "the linguistic supports of an immoral social system" that Faulkner "self-consciously analyze[s]" in most of his major novels (Snead x).

2   It is interesting that Morrison in *Playing in the Dark* offers analyses of the fiction of Cather, Poe, and Hemingway, but not of Faulkner, though her 1955 M.A. thesis was written on Faulkner and Virginia Woolf. Introducing a 1985 reading of *Beloved,* then a work in progress, at the annual Faulkner and Yoknapatawpha Conference in Oxford, Morrison commented on Faulkner in ways that pointed ahead to some of her concerns in *Playing in the Dark.* Her reasons, she said, for "being interested and deeply moved by all his subjects had something to do with [her] desire to find out something about this country and that artistic articulation of its past that was not available in history, which is what art and fiction can do but sometimes history refuses to do" (Morrison, "Faulkner and Women," 296).

3   In his introduction to *"Race," Writing and Difference,* Gates argues:

> The sense of difference defined in popular usages of the term "race" has both described and *inscribed* differences of language, belief system, artistic tradition, and gene pool, as well as all sorts of supposedly natural attributes such as rhythm, athletic ability, cerebration, usury, fidelity, and so forth. The relation of "racial character" and these sorts of characteristics has been inscribed through tropes of race, lending the sanction of God, biology, or the natural order to even presumably unbiased descriptions of cultural tendencies and differences. (Gates, 5)

4   In a 1990 essay on the women of *Go Down, Moses,* Elisabeth Muhlenfeld writes that she can find no single article on any of the women in the book (Muhlenfeld 211). Muhlenfeld herself argues that the women of the novel "carry great artistic weight" (Muhlenfeld 199), although she seems to agree with Philip Weinstein's assessment that the female characters "have no instigating power" and are tragically passive objects of white male desire (Weinstein 183). In her 1994 study *Faulkner and Southern Womanhood,* Diane Roberts' discussion of Faulkner's representations of women in *Go*

Down, Moses in terms of the cultural stereotypes of the tragic mulatta and mammy raises provocative questions of the text such as, "Where does desire intersect with subjugation? When does 'black' become 'white,' or, using the preferred image of the purity-obsessed South, when does the "drop of ink" pollute the clean white page?" (Roberts 79)

5   Mine is a different approach from that of Susan Stanford Friedman who in her essay "Spatialization: A Strategy for Reading Narrative" visualizes two axes in narrative: the horizontal, which has to do with what happens in the story (plot, character, action, closure, etc.), and the vertical, which she relates to multiple resonances of a text, whether they be cultural, intertextual, psychodynamic, and so forth.

6   In *The Spatiality of the Novel*, Joseph A. Kestner argues, in fact, that the interpretive act is itself spatial, "for the text creates a 'genidentic' field, incorporating the reader in a dynamic relation with it" (Kestner 22).

7   The engraving is reproduced in Gilman, 239.

8   In *Faulkner and Southern Womanhood*, which focuses on Faulkner's use of female stereotypes, Roberts employs the Bakhtinian concept of the "grotesque body" to explore representations of black women in general and the mammy figure in particular "as white southern culture understood them" and as Faulkner created them (Roberts xv). She elaborates on the relation between body, race, and gender in literary representations of the mammy in *The Myth of Aunt Jemima*.

9   Sundquist believes that "the ledgers, like Benjy's section in *The Sound and the Fury*, are a concentrated representation, a mysterious and seemingly sacred account, of acts and passions whose symbolic value draws into itself and envelops the interpretations it necessitates" (Sundquist 137). John T. Matthews finds in Ike's reading and writing in the ledgers an effort "to confront and to contradict his grandfather" (Matthews 264). I see the ledgers in terms of Morrison's theory of Africanist narrative and American literature, as the highly claustrophobic space of "bound blackness" written by white men and functioning as a site of contemplation and exorcism for white men.

10   In *The Feminine and Faulkner: Reading (Beyond) Sexual Difference*, I associate this excessiveness of Faulkner's texts with the dismantling of oppositional ways of conceptualizing gender.

11   For a discussion of Faulkner's statements about racial issues, see

Charles Peavy's *Go Slow Now: Faulkner and the Race Question.* Donald Petesch discusses the relationship of the fiction to the statements in "Faulkner on Negroes: The Conflict between the Public Man and the Private Art."

12 The "Delta Autumn" woman is nameless throughout the various versions of the story – in manuscript and in its published form as a short story in *Story* (published after *Go Down, Moses* but written first). See Joanne V. Creighton, *William Faulkner's Craft of Revision,* for a complete description of Faulkner's revisions in *Go Down, Moses.*

WORKS CITED

Butler, Octavia. *Kindred.* Boston: Beacon, 1979.

Collins, Patricia Hill. *Black Feminist Thought: Knowledge, Consciousness, and the Politics of Empowerment.* New York: Routledge, 1990.

Creighton, Joanne V. *William Faulkner's Craft of Revision.* Detroit: Wayne State University Press, 1977.

Davis, Angela. *Women, Race and Class.* New York: Random House, 1981.

Davis, Thadious M. *Faulkner's "Negro": Art and the Southern Context.* Baton Rouge: Louisiana State University Press, 1983.

Faulkner, William. *Absalom, Absalom!* New York: Modern Library, 1966.

Go Down, Moses. New York: Vintage, 1990.

Friedman, Susan Stanford. "Spatialization: A Strategy for Reading Narrative." *Narrative* 1, 1 (1990): 12–23.

Gates, Henry Louis, Jr. "Writing 'Race' and the Difference It Makes." In (ed.) *"Race," Writing and Difference.* Chicago: University of Chicago Press, 1986, 1–20.

Gilman, Sander L. "Black Bodies, White Bodies: Toward an Iconography of Female Sexuality in Late Nineteenth-Century Art, Medicine, and Literature." In Gates, ed., *"Race," Writing and Difference,* 223–261.

Gwin, Minrose C. *Black and White Women of the Old South: The Peculiar Sisterhood in American Literature.* Knoxville: University of Tennessee Press, 1985.

The Feminine and Faulkner: Reading (Beyond) Sexual Difference. Knoxville: University of Tennessee Press, 1990.

Harris, Trudier. *From Mammies to Militants: Domestics in Black American Literature.* Philadelphia: Temple University Press, 1982.

Irigaray, Luce. *This Sex Which Is Not One.* Ithaca: Cornell University Press, 1985.

Jacobs, Harriet A. [Linda Brent]. *Incidents in the Life of a Slave Girl,* ed. Jean Fagan Yellin. Cambridge: Harvard University Press, 1987.

Jenkins, Lee. *Faulkner and Black-White Relations: A Psychoanalytic Approach.* New York: Columbia University Press, 1981.

Kestner, Joseph. *The Spatiality of the Novel.* Detroit: Wayne State University Press, 1978.

Matthews, John T. *The Play of Faulkner's Language.* Ithaca: Cornell University Press, 1982.

Mohanty, Chandra Talpale. "Introduction: Cartographies of Struggle: Third World Women and the Politics of Feminism." In *Third World Women and the Politics of Feminism,* ed. Mohanty, Ann Russo, and Lourdes Torres. Bloomington: Indiana University Press, 1991.

Moore, Henrietta L. *Space, Text and Gender: An Anthropological Study of the Marakwet of Kenya.* Cambridge: Cambridge University Press, 1986.

Morrison, Toni. *Beloved.* New York: New American Library, 1988.

"Faulkner and Women." In *Faulkner and Women: Faulkner and Yoknapatawpha, 1985,* ed. Doreen Fowler and Ann J. Abadie. Jackson: University Press of Mississippi, 1986, 295–302.

Playing in the Dark: Whiteness and the Literary Imagination. Cambridge: Harvard University Press, 1990.

Muhlenfeld, Elisabeth. "The Distaff Side: The Women of *Go Down, Moses.*" In *Critical Essays on William Faulkner: The McCaslin Family,* ed. Arthur F. Kinney. Boston: G. K. Hall, 1990, 198–211.

Peavy, Charles D. *Go Slow Now: Faulkner and the Race Question.* Eugene: University of Oregon Press, 1971.

Petesch, Donald. "Faulkner on Negroes: The Conflict between the Public Man and the Private Art." *Southern Humanities Review* 10 (1976): 55–64.

Roberts, Diane. *Faulkner and Southern Womanhood.* Athens: University of Georgia Press, 1994.

The Myth of Aunt Jemima. London: Routledge, 1994.

Snead, James A. *Figures of Division: William Faulkner's Major Novels.* New York: Methuen, 1986.

Sundquist, Eric J. *Faulkner: The House Divided.* Baltimore: Johns Hopkins University Press, 1983.

Weinstein, Philip M. "Marginalia: Faulkner's Black Lives." In *Faulkner and Race: Faulkner and Yoknapatawpha, 1986,* ed. Doreen Fowler and Ann J. Abadie. Jackson: University Press of Mississippi, 1987.

Weisman, Leslie. *Discrimination by Design: A Feminist Critique of the Man-Made Environment.* Chicago: University of Illinois Press, 1992.

Williams, Patricia J. *The Alchemy of Race and Rights.* Cambridge: Harvard University Press, 1991.

5

Who Wears the Mask? Memory, Desire, and Race in *Go Down, Moses*

JUDITH L. SENSIBAR

I BEGIN with these questions: Why "Pantaloon in Black"? Why, twenty years after Faulkner had abandoned his first Laforguean persona and with it those numerous and explicit evocations of the *commedia* and of the protean Pierrot – the dominant voice of his long self-apprenticeship to poetry – does he (in what many consider the culminating moment in his career as a novelist),[1] explicitly invoke the language and persona of his literary childhood? Why does the structural conception of *Go Down, Moses* also hark back to those years as Faulkner realizes in prose the elliptical and lyrical form of his early poem sequences?[2] What do these haunted and haunting *commedia* figures from his difficult and protracted years as a would-be poet have to do with a suicidally grieving black mill worker from Yoknapatawpha County? Why, in short, in a novel about loss and mourning,[3] does Faulkner return to this ghost from his own imaginative life? And why, now, is he figured as black? What do Faulkner's choices signal about the power of memory and, in particular, the power of the memory of interracial love, in the deeply conflicted and racially charged cultural terrain of his own North Mississippi between 1865 and 1940 and in a novel set in that same spatial and temporal time frame? What does the language of these memories say about the pervasive need for this particular south-

This essay was begun during my tenure as a fellow at the Virginia Foundation for the Humanities, Charlottesville, Virginia, in the spring of 1993, and was completed under a National Endowment for the Humanities Fellowship for University Teachers (1993–94). I am grateful to both institutions for providing me the time to work on the book of which this essay is a part.

ern white male writing fiction in 1941 to assume a certain kind of masking?

Such questions cannot be answered in one brief essay. Therefore, let us suggest some directions of inquiry. Establishing their efficacy involves a series of linkages – autobiographical, historical, cultural, psychological, genealogical, and intertextual. My perspective is essentially psychoanalytic and feminist and my basic method is close reading of a variety of related texts. I am seeking a fuller understanding of a crucial moment in Faulkner's five-decades-long imaginative engagement with the forces and fields of cultural intermingling and of cross-racial embrace and exploitation that underwrite the racial conflicts forming the crucible, and thus the structural and emotional matrix, of his best fiction. These speculations will, I hope, help to unearth the complex negotiations behind one of Faulkner's most self-revealing texts. I see the artist's perception and representation of racial cultures, black and white, as permanently dependent and therefore constantly threatened by and subject to destabilization, a destabilization figured so vividly in this novel whose form itself constantly threatens to implode.

In reading *Go Down, Moses,* particularly its "Pantaloon in Black" section, through the rich political, emotional, and cultural landscape of Faulkner's life, I want first to suggest a relation between the chapter's meanings in the novel and Faulkner's earliest recorded racially figured memory.[4] Like many of the obsessive racially and sexually charged fantasies of his fictional young white southern men, it is coded white. Writing home from Paris to his favorite great-aunt 'Bama McLean in September 1925, he says he is looking forward to the arrival of a relative his mother's age:

I will be awfully glad to see Vannye again. The last time I remember seeing her was when I was 3, I suppose. I had gone to spend the night with Aunt Willie (in Ripley) and I was suddenly taken with one of those spells of loneliness and nameless sorrow that children suffer, for what or because of what they do not know. And Vannye and Natalie brought me home, with a kerosene lamp. I remember how Vannye's hair looked in the light – like honey. Vannye was impersonal; quite aloof: she was holding the lamp. Natalie was quick and dark. She was touching me. She must have carried me.[5]

An alert reader immediately picks up on the two culturally constructed binaries Faulkner invokes here to describe what he
claims as his three-year-old memory of the racially inscribed feminine. Vannye, the golden girl whom he anticipates as soft and
sweet, a sweetness he licks with his tongue in the lyrical "ls" of her
hair looking in the lamplight like honey but whom he experiences
in the next brutally abrupt sentence as "impersonal; quite aloof."
And Natalie: "quick" and "dark," sensuous ("touching me. She
must have carried me.") – in essence, both nurturing and sexual.[6]
Throughout his life, this memory will serve Faulkner's imagination as a core or organizing fantasy. He continually mines its repressed content, drawing on those materials for the increasingly
rich and complex fantasies that inform the troubled conjunctions
of race and sexuality in much of his fiction. Its most fully elaborated expression and attendant conflicts are realized in *Go Down,
Moses* where identification with, desire for, and fear of the feminine are irremediably linked with race, gender, and the maternal
in every male character's quest for identity and selfhood.

But before considering one of the roles this fantasy plays in *Go
Down, Moses,* let us establish its genealogy by discussing briefly a
single moment of its figuration in an earlier novel. On reading
Faulkner's screen memory, anyone familiar with *The Sound and
the Fury* is reminded of Quentin's white and black constructions
of female sexuality, most specifically the "dirty," "black," and
"friendly" little Italian girl in the "Land of the kike home of the
wop" (*The Sound and the Fury,* hereafter SF: 155) whom he calls
"sister" and who reminds him of a childhood sexual initiation
with another Other "in the high sweet emptiness" of his father's
barn, a place hidden from the prying eyes of his real sister, her
white counterpart. Quentin calls this other a "dirty girl." Naming
her Natalie, Faulkner invokes his own first memory of being
touched and held by a dark woman under the light (sight?) or
direction of a honey-haired but aloof white woman:

There? Touching her
Not there
There? not raining hard but we couldnt hear anything but the roof and as if it
was my blood or her blood

. . . Did Caddy go away did she go to the house you cant see the barn from our house. (SF 167)

Here the forbidden and dangerous yet deeply erotic quality of blackness is made explicit as Quentin elides images of sweetness, touch, secretiveness, dark, and dirty with sexual excitement and the mingling and merging of his (understood white) body and blood with "dirty" Natalie's:

Its like dancing sitting down did you ever dance sitting down did you ever dance sitting down? We could hear the rain, a rat in the crib, the empty barn vacant with horses. How do you hold to dance do you hold like this
    Oh
I used to hold like this you thought I wasnt strong enough didn't you
    Oh Oh Oh Oh
    I hold to use like this I mean did you hear what I said I said
    Oh Oh Oh Oh (SF 168)[7]

Here, the gradual looosening and then disintegration of syntax and merging of the two voices figures the disintegration of body boundaries. It lasts only a moment. Quentin cuts off his fantasy and jerks himself into the bleak and sterile present where "The road went on still and empty, the sun slanting more and more" where, turning his gaze outward to the dark and dirty and sweet little Italian girl, he still grasps for the tattered remnants of memory and desire: "Her stiff little pigtails were bound at the tips with bits of crimson cloth. A corner of the wrapping flapped a little as she walked, the nose of the loaf naked" (SF 168).

Quentin's fear of the white female gaze, his agony, his inability to permit himself to satisfy his desire, his need to punish this "blackness" in himself, derives from his equation, learned from his sexually repressed and racist parents – his cold, hypochondriacal, and rigidly conventional mother and his equally conventional, remote, and alcoholic father – that to feel erotic pleasure is indeed to be black, a transformation, I will argue, Faulkner achieves in a highly coded form in *Go Down, Moses*, the book of mourning written after the death of his own black "mother" and dedicated to her.[8] But because this transformation, like the early idealizing love that fuels it, is taboo, it must always be punished.

To be black, as Quentin's fantasies so vividly illustrate – "trampling my shadow's bones into the concrete with hard heels" (SF148) – is to enter "the dungeon [which] was mother herself," to "not be" (SF 215,216). Quentin's fear and his mirroring desire operate at both oedipal and pre-oedipal levels. His fear of, and forbidden desire for, not castration but total annihilation, if he enters this inviting yet suffocating prison of blackness – that is, his racialized pre-oedipal fear – causes him to kill himself. Perhaps what Quentin really fears is that if he gives in to his desire to enter into and to merge with his black mother/Natalie – in a word, the feminine conceived as sexual, as black – he will erase his white self.

In "Pantaloon in Black," where the authorial voice dons a *commedia* mask from his literary childhood to slip inside a mythically endowed young man with skin the same blue-black color as that of his recently dead black "Mammy," his erotic desire is momentarily unmediated by fear.[9] But because Faulkner, a white southern man born in 1897, ultimately cannot imagine erotic desire as anything other than taboo and always identifies it with blackness and the feminine in this racialized culture, he has to destroy his black mask, Rider.

" 'Mammys' . . . became second mothers
to white children."[10]

Caroline Barr, the African-American woman to whom Faulkner dedicated *Go Down, Moses,* and who died in January 1940, came to work for his parents, Maud and Murry Falkner, some time before September 1902 when she moved with them and their three young boys from Ripley to Oxford, Mississippi.[11] According to Faulkner's daughter, Jill Summers, Barr had been a "house servant" of her great-grandparents before William was born. Then she joined the Falkner household.[12] William was her only charge until shortly before his second birthday when his brother Murry (Jack) was born. Thus, for the first two years of his life, he had the exclusive attention of two mothers, one white and one black. Summers gives her sense of some aspects of her father's relationship with the woman who had cared for him from infancy and who, in 1933, came to care for his only child: "The women Pappy most loved and admired were Aunt 'Bama, Granny [Maud Falkner], and Mammy Callie. . . . Mammie Callie meant the most to him. She was independent, positive, and self-sufficient. Physically, they reminded me of each other. . . . They were all small. Mammy Callie was the biggest. All three were wiry, tough, little ladies."[13] Unlike Callie Barr, however, his mother was not emotionally or physically demonstrative. Again Jill Summers:

There was very little warmth in Granny. I think that Mammy Callie took her place in Pappy's life. Mammy had been his mother, his nurse, his teacher, and everything else for so long. She was the only person in the world who's ever called Pappy a nickname, that I know.[14]

To return to the imagery of Faulkner's three-year-old screen memory, although Natalie's sister Vannye held the light (meaning perhaps the power of whiteness), she remained emotionally aloof.[15] Both the triangulation and the split and doubling aspects of Faulkner's intrapsychic relations with Maud and Callie Barr appear reflected in this screen memory of two sisters, one dark and one light. It was a memory to which Faulkner's imagination often returned as he invented his fictional black and white mothers, lovers, and sisters.

What was the nature of Faulkner's earliest experiences with the black and white women who mothered him in a world governed by apparently rigid sexual and racial hierarchies and boundaries? How did the reality that, within his own family, these boundaries appeared extraordinarily permeable, affect him? (Certainly we see that paradoxical rigidity and permeability refracted in much of Faulkner's fiction, including *Go Down, Moses*.) For example, Faulkner's brother Jack writes " 'Mammys' . . . became second mothers to white children." The inscription Faulkner had carved on Barr's grave: "MAMMY/ Her white children/ bless her," supports this assertion. It also signifies her white children's exclusive ownership, even in death and even in the black cemetery. But such claims, which ignore black kinship ties, also reveal the dehumanization that ownership of other human beings necessitates. This dehumanization is a constant and constantly conflicted subject of Faulkner's fictional texts. According to Jack Falkner, Caroline Barr "was big in will power and a sense of right and wrong, but Mother always had the last say."[16] As Faulkner's white mother Maud Falkner noted approvingly, "Callie knew her place."

Simultaneously invested with and stripped of moral authority, Barr was also demonized by her white employers and "her white children" as the stereotypic black female – a creature of ungovernable and undiscriminating sexual appetites: "She would suddenly take off with some man she had run across in one way or another," another brother wrote, causing their father to go chasing often into the next state to bring her home when she tired of her lover.[17] Yet the Falkner brothers knew, and it was common knowledge in Oxford, that both of their grandfathers kept black mistresses for whom one even left his white wife. What was Caroline Barr's "place" in the two worlds between which she constantly negotiated – her own family and Maud and Murry Falkner's, where she cared for four white boys and, when he was drunk, their father?

That, and the question of his own "place" in relation to her, is the masked and encoded subject of "Pantaloon in Black" as it is, less opaquely, in sections like "The Fire and the Hearth." Still seeking for words to explore and articulate a screen memory that occurred perhaps before he had mastered language, Faulkner here gives a similar experience to a white boy whose biological mother died in childbirth on a "spring night of flood and isolation." The shift Faulkner makes into the camouflage of fiction allows him to articulate clearly the child's idealizing identification:

Even before he was out of infancy the two houses had become interchangeable: himself and his foster-brother sleeping on the same pallet in the white man's house or in the same bed in the negro's and eating of the same food at the same table in either, actually preferring the negro house, the hearth on which even in summer a little fire burned, centering the life in it, to his own. It did not even need to come to him as a part of his family's chronicle that his white father and his foster-brother's black one had done the same; *it never occurred to him that they in their turn and simultaneously had not had the first of remembering projected upon a single woman whose skin was likewise dark.* One day he knew, without wondering or remembering how he had learned that either, that the black woman was not his mother, and did not regret it; he knew that his own mother was dead and did not grieve. There was still the black woman, constant, steadfast, and the black man of whom he saw as much and even more than his own father. (110, my italics)

Here, in the boy Carothers' simultaneous acknowledgment of his mirroring relationship with "the only mother he would remember," a recognition of his deep and abiding identification with her, and his denial that it meant anything, Faulkner clarifies the psychic form that denial takes. To identify not only with the feminine but with the black feminine is so shameful and so taboo that the feeling part of the self has to be killed. That loss, because one is never permitted to mourn for it, is felt always as a loss. Carothers Edmonds suffers permanent damage.[18] He will spend his life seeking revenge, doomed to repeat that first loss which he had been taught he was not permitted to feel. That is one reason why in "Delta Autumn" he abandons his "black" lover and their infant son. In "Pantaloon in Black," donning the mask of blackface (the pantaloon, Rider), Faulkner further explores the meaning of that loss. But his exploration throughout this novel and throughout the record of *his writing* of this novel is, as always, fraught with an ambivalence often articulated as blatant racism.

"The old matriarch who raised me"

Explaining why he was late in returning the galleys for *The Hamlet*, Faulkner wrote his Random House editor Robert Haas that, on the last day of January 1940, Caroline Barr, "the old matriarch who raised me died suddenly from a stroke" and "so I have had little of heart or time either for work."[19] Yet he was already continuing to fictionalize her life and had begun fictionalizing her death in what would become *Go Down, Moses*. This book is, in some ways, his most intimate and startling report on the degree to which the underlying instability and permeability of the codes and conventions that dominated his public and private discourse on race were reflected in, fueled, and structured his imaginative vision.[20]

Two days later Faulkner responded to Haas's sympathy note and enclosure. The latter was probably *The New York Times* account of the eulogy he had written and delivered to Callie Barr's family and friends at a gathering he and his wife Estelle held in their parlor prior to the black funeral service for Caroline Barr at what was then called the Negro Baptist Church in Oxford and the burial ceremonies later that afternoon in the black section of St. Peter's cemetery. He sent Haas the polished version of Barr's eulogy, parts of which he later used verbatim in the third section of "The Fire and the Hearth."[21] In an accompanying note he wrote, "This is what I said and when I got it on paper afterward, it turned out to be pretty good prose."[22]

The literal space in which the eulogy was delivered – the Faulkners' parlor – the inspiration for its composition and its later use, and the small ambivalences masked by the conventional rhetoric of the white master's eulogy to his faithful servant, "the matriarch who raised me," serve as part of the foundation for my argument: that *Go Down, Moses* offers the clearest genealogy of its author's own racial unconscious. The novel's elliptical shape is a return to and a repetition of Faulkner's earliest narrative experiments, his poem sequences of the teens and early twenties. But this is a repetition with a difference; narrative gaps enclose its kelson, "Pantaloon in Black," the section that just won't fit, where Faulkner brings to formal fruition a coded poetics he has been developing since the beginning of his writing career, to articulate his vision of the racial politics of his North Mississippi culture. He signals this in his deliberately decentered and apparently unconnected third section, "Pantaloon in Black," where he returns, as he has in a more guarded fashion throughout his fictional career, to his talismanic earliest narrative persona, Pierrot/Pantaloon, to house the form and give shape to what Eric Lott calls "the white racial unconscious" and to explore its origins in his own split maternal. This maternal is composed of all the paradoxes and contradictions that mark both the black "Mammy" figure and the Southern (white) Lady.[23]

This dual mothering produces the black/white *commedia* trickster figure which Faulkner adopted as his first narrative persona and which he resurrects in "Pantaloon in Black."

Much of Faulkner's racial unconscious springs (like that of most white middle- and upper-class Mississippians of his generation), from his doubly mothered childhood.[24] Cultural conventions prevented him from ever fully acknowledging one of the two women who nurtured him.[25] Often they required that she be demeaned. In contrast to Faulkner's eulogy for Caroline Barr, a public act conforming to those conventions, *Go Down, Moses*, a fiction, is both an act of true mourning and, in rare unguarded moments, of the liberation that true mourning brings. The mask of art permits Faulkner to articulate those conventions and explore the history of his complicity in them and the confusions, desire, hatred, and pain they cause. The masks and theater generated by those conventions are vividly represented in Rider's mourning as, like his author, he makes "his own prints" in the dust where Mannie had walked each week, "setting the period now as he strode on . . . breasting the air her body had vacated, his eyes touching the objects . . . her eyes had lost" (137). They are equally present in the homosocial and homoerotic world of the hunt where another encoded version of his African-American mother, the half-Choctaw half-black Sam Fathers, mothers the white boy. The boy experiences the warmth of Sam's body "the two of them wrapped in the damp, warm, negro-rank quilt while the wilderness closed behind his entrance" creating a womb-like "fluid circumambiance, drowsing, earless, almost lightless" so that it seemed to the boy "that at the age of ten he was witnessing his own birth" (195).

Yet, the novel does not cohere in any formal high modernist sense; rather, it deliberately does not cohere and "Pantaloon in Black" tells why. Furthermore, the section warns that the only way the novel *will* cohere is in its systematic revelations about the ways in which race is figured and about how those figurations work to split communities apart. John Limon argues that in "Pantaloon in Black" "Faulkner has formed a text in the image of a Southern Negro and invited us to join an interpretive community on the model of Yoknapatawpha County."[26] I would argue rather that, like the white actors and white audiences of minstrel shows, with which he was familiar, Faulkner has formed a text, Rider, the Pantaloon, in the image of what Eric Lott would call his own racial unconscious, the Rider/writer who mourns over the grave of his beloved Mannie/Mammy, "a grave marked off without order about the barren plot by shards of pottery and broken bottles and old brick and other objects insignificant to sight but actually of a profound meaning and fatal to touch, which no white man could have read."[27] This is precisely the point. The problem with this novel is that Faulkner does not want to read what he is writing. As Ralph Ellison, from whom some of Lott's argument derives, explains:

The mask was the thing (the "thing" in more ways than one) and its function was to veil the humanity of Negroes thus reduced to a sign, and to repress the white audience's awareness of its moral identification with its own acts and with the human ambiguities pushed behind the mask. . . . When the white man steps behind the mask of the trickster his freedom is circumscribed by the fear that he is not simply miming a personification of his disorder and chaos but that he will become in fact that which he intends to symbolize; that he will be trapped somewhere in the mystery of hell (for there is a mystery in the whiteness of blackness, the innocence of evil and the evil of innocence, . . .) and thus lose that freedom which . . . he would recognize as the white man's alone.[28]

This circumscription of the white trickster reveals itself in the next note Faulkner wrote Haas five months after Caroline Barr's death:

Do you want to consider a collection of short stories, most of them from magazines since 33 or 34, perhaps one or two unpublished yet? Could get it together in a month.

Also, Ober has four stories about niggers, I can build onto them, write some more, make a book like THE UNVANQUISHED, could get it together in six months perhaps.

Among these four was "Pantaloon in Black," which Faulkner had sent to his agent in March of 1940, less than two months after Barr's death.[29] Masking his emotional involvement and yet revealing the dual consciousness with which he approached his project in the apparently demeaning and self-demeaning racist epithet describing it to his eastern publisher, Faulkner was already well into his private eulogy. Yet, I wonder, are the "niggers" to whom he refers here only in his stories, or is Faulkner including himself as well? Up against the authority of his New York publisher, is he dropping into blackface here for reasons similar to Lucas Beauchamp's who "Without changing the inflection of his voice and apparently without effort or even design . . . became not Negro but nigger, not secret so much as impenetrable, not servile and not effacing, but enveloping himself in an aura of timeless and stupid impassivity almost like a smell" (60). Faulkner needed money desperately. By the end of April he wrote Haas that he'd have to postpone work on it "since the chapters which I have written and tried to sell as short stories have not sold."[30]

It turned out to be a difficult year. As usual, he was strapped for funds: "I'm so busy borrowing money from Random House," he wrote his agent at the end of May, that "I dont even have time to write."[31] Yet by November, in the ten months since Callie Barr's death, he had completed all of *Go Down, Moses* but "The Bear." He took off to the Delta for his annual hunting trip with the usual crowd. There, perhaps reliving Rider's vain attempt to dull thinking and feeling with bootleg liquor, he nearly died of acute alcohol poisoning.[32] But perhaps also, his drinking and hunting served as a violent but private and wordless negation of the romanticized role he had given them – the lie "the boy" spoke in "The Bear," which, like the other hunts in this novel, proposes that what makes a (white) man is not a relationship, but a ritual killing (176, 178), and that appears to perpetuate a romantic myth that men in the Edenic wilderness are beyond racism (176, 178, 191):

There was always a bottle present, so that it would seem to him that those fine fierce instants of heart and brain and courage and wiliness and speed were concentrated and distilled into that brown liquor which not women, not boys and children, but only hunters drank, drinking not of the blood they spilled but some condensation of the wild immortal spirit, . . . drinking it moderately, humbly even. (192)[33]

Not until May 1941 did he mention *Go Down, Moses* again. Now the racial epithet was gone. In the intervening months his project had blossomed and paid off; he had sold short story versions of everything but "The Bear," increasing his confidence in the interest of his subject. Although still anxious about marketability, he now abandoned his defensive stance:

Last year I mentioned a volume, collected short stories, general theme being relationship between white and negro races here. . . . Do present conditions warrant such a book? That is, do you want to publish such a book; and will it do enough to ease the financial situation between us for me to get at it. . . . I do not want to gamble the time and effort of getting this mss. into shape unless it will really benefit me?[34]

In January 1942, more than two years after Caroline Barr's death, Faulkner sent Haas the dedication for his tenth novel:

TO MAMMY
CAROLINE BARR
MISSISSIPPI
[1840–1940]
Who was born in slavery and who gave
to my family a fidelity without
stint or calculation of recompense
and to my childhood an immeasur-
able devotion and love   (SL, 148)

By the end of March 1942, *Go Down, Moses* was in the book-stores and Faulkner told Haas, with the characteristic understatement he had reserved for good work (both his own and others) since the early twenties, that the book was "all right. It will pull its weight" (SL 149). As his letters tell, Faulkner's financial situation was the initiating and major external exigency driving the production of this novel. Was there a market out there, he had asked his publisher, when he first proposed it. The novel's dedication, Faulkner's public statement about his feelings for Barr, falls within and so perpetuates the convention of white masters' eulogies for faithful black slaves (and later, servants). It repeats phrases from his eulogy. Narratively, as a framing device, it functions as an introduction to and extension of its fictions.[35]

In this sense, the inscription closes down his novel before it even begins. Is it, too, a mask? One that signals its author's inability to escape the constructions of his racialized culture?[36]

Let us go back to this novel's beginnings, turning to Faulkner's original, or rather, not so original, eulogy and the space and circumstances under which it was delivered and received.

> Caroline has known me all my life. It was my privilege to see her out of hers. After my father's death, to Mammy I came to represent the head of that family to which she had given a half a century of fidelity and devotion. But the relation between us never became that of master and servant. She still remained one of my earliest recollections, not only as a person, but as a fount of authority over my conduct and of security for my physical welfare, and of active and constant affection and love. She was an active and constant precept for decent behavior. From her I learned to tell the truth, to refrain from waste, to be considerate of the weak and respectful of age. I saw fidelity to a family which was not hers, devotion and love for people she had not borne.
>
> She was born in bondage with a dark skin and most of her early maturity passed in a dark and tragic time for the land of her birth. She went through vicissitudes which she had not caused; she assumed cares and griefs which were not even her cares and griefs. She was paid wages for this, but pay is still just money. And she never received very much of that, so she never laid up anything of this world's goods. Yet she accepted that too without cavil or calculation or complaint, so that by that very failure she earned the gratitude and affection of the family she had conferred fidelity and devotion upon, and gained the grief and regret of the aliens who loved and lost her.
>
> She was born and lived and served, and died and now is mourned; if there is a heaven, she has gone there.[37]

Faulkner delivered this eulogy at a service he held for Caroline Barr's family, but their presence in his speech (where Faulkner uses the word "family" or its equivalent five times), is noted only by its absence. The only family he mentions is his own.

Barr's relatives were grateful for some of Faulkner's efforts. Her great-niece, Rachel Mc Geehee who is now in her eighties, recalls:

When she died, he [Faulkner] called me and I got my sister and we went 'cross the Bailey Woods (we call it Bailey Woods), from South

Eighth Street that is hitting Bailey Woods – we went 'cross there and the snow was on the ground. It was cold – ice and stuff. We went 'cross the field and Mr. Faulkner told us he would furnish *everything* and we called Bankhead [Funeral Home]. And they took care Aunt Callie and I had her bonnet made in Clyde Bolden [shop]. They furnished *everything* and I mean it. It wasn't no poor person stuff you know. And then he had the funeral in the living room! In his living room. And I think he had the Community Choir of Oxford. I think they call that choir to come down and sing and then he let us brought her to the Baptist Church. He come with it [the body]. His and Miss Estelle had the funeral and carried her on out there and buried her.[38]

Faulkner's biographers interpret this moment as indicative of the author's love and respect, a moment of great honor for Caroline Barr. Certainly, from the Faulkners' perspective, it was. Caroline Barr's relatives see differently, however. They believe that had Faulkner really meant to honor her, he should have given his eulogy in *their* church. In a later interview, Mrs. Mc Geehee's daughter, Mildred Quarles, provided the subtext of her mother's account. Quarles explained:

"It was awful that he had it in his parlor. William said he was gonna have it at his house and they had her [Callie Barr] in his parlor! You know, white folk call it parlor. In his parlor! My mother and Aunt Dora told me some things you don't do. And my mother and all of them told me about William speaking over Aunt Callie. One aunt, she said 'Hell, he drunk. He don't know any better than to have it in the parlor.' "[39]

As you might expect, Faulkner's eulogy, like the inscription he placed on Callie Barr's tombstone, conforms fairly closely to the genre of eulogies written by masters to memorialize their favorite slaves.

In *Go Down, Moses* Faulkner returns to this eulogy in several instances. Each time he draws from it, he shifts from critique and rupture into sentimentality. Thus, from a rhetorical and narrative perspective, invoking Barr's eulogy is a reactionary move. For example, in "The Fire and the Hearth," the flashback scene in which Molly punishes the young Edmonds by giving him what he asked for when, at age seven, he suddenly began treating the black family who had raised him "as a subject race" (171), is followed by the grown Edmonds' ruminations, in the present, as he contemplates "the breaking up after forty-five years the home of the woman who had been the only mother" he ever knew. Edmonds' recital of Molly's qualities reads like a catalogue of the positive conventional character traits one claims for one's "mammy." One might try to read it ironically, except that Molly herself is sentimentalized and stereotyped throughout this section. The language with which Faulkner introduces it is the language of Callie Barr's eulogy. Molly becomes once more

the only mother he, Edmonds, ever knew, who had surrounded him always with care for his physical body and for his spirit too, teaching him his manners, behavior – to be gentle with his inferiors, honorable with his equals, generous to the weak and considerate of the aged, courteous, truthful and brave to all – who had given him, the motherless, without stint or expectation of reward that constant and abiding devotion and love which existed nowhere else in this world for him. (117)

With this set piece Faulkner succeeds in throwing into serious question the significance of the lesson Molly had supposedly taught the child Edmonds about honor, courtesy, and simple human decency. As he makes his relationship with her into a set piece, he physically transforms her to a static, doll-like figure: "She sat . . . motionless, her tiny gnarled hands immobile again on the white apron, the shrunken and tragic mask touched here and there into highlight by the fire" (119). As Edmonds says, "Then it was as if it had never happened at all" (113). Sentimentalism operates here in the same two-pronged manner that it functions in the songs associated with minstrel shows, songs with a remarkably long afterlife, such as Al Jolson's rendition of "Mammy" in *The Jazz Singer*.[40] It simultaneously exalts and murders. What Eric Lott calls "the vogue of the dear departed" Ann Douglas established as a "cornerstone of sentimentalism . . . the Christian exaltation of the powerless," as a way of justifying and naturalizing slavery. Such eulogizing was always over the death of an other – dead women and dead male and female slaves. Lott reads the repetition of this theme in nineteenth-century blackface minstrelsy "as a form of racial and sexual aggression, that is, metaphorical murder." Its purpose was to bury "the whole lamented business of slavery" by eliminating "black people themselves."[41] In *Go Down, Moses* invocations by white male characters of Callie Barr's eulogy ("the social configuration of the elegized black woman") function similarly. They close down the narrative.

Yet Rider's mourning in "Pantaloon in Black" has the opposite effect. To create Rider, Faulkner invokes what seems at first an equally stultifying convention, his earliest persona, an alienated *pierrotiste*, to enact a story of mourning that denies the efficacy of eulogy. Coding Rider as his originary poetic voice, he fuses his identity with his character's.[42] Faulkner, the becoming artist, and Rider, the becoming man and mythmaker, are one. The Mannie that Rider mourns is both his mother and his tabooed lover, Caroline Barr and the self he fears the loss of in losing her as well as the self he fears to acknowledge.[43] She is indeed a ghost. Thus the linguistic play in Mannie's dually gendered name; thus Rider's constant attempts to "touch" and merge with her traces – her dust, her shadow, her shade.

Faulkner seems here to be suggesting that his imaginative impulses and vision spring, in part, from his identification with his "mammy" as, in this highly coded way, he momentarily moves, through Rider, into a zone of feeling and experience where no one else can follow. This is why only blacks can read the memorials on Mannie's grave and why no one in Rider's community, either black or white (except the ghost of Mannie), can understand him. Rider deliberately marginalizes and ultimately obliterates himself from the text. In doing so he creates a powerful myth – the story of his grief – that his community will never forget.[44]

Rider's rage and grief at Mannie's death is beyond his control. No language can express it; thus his body speaks. Mourning the lost maternal, he returns to the presymbolic. All his senses take command to speak an image of the body in pain and conflict. When he tries to eat, to nurture himself with food she once cooked for him, he gags: "the congealed and lifeless mass seemed to bounce on contact with his lips . . . peas and spoon spattered and rang upon the plate; his chair crashed backward, and he was standing, feeling the muscles of his jaw beginning to drag his mouth open, tugging toward the top half of his head. But he stopped that too before it became sound, *holding himself* again while he rapidly scraped the food from his plate" (141–142, my italics). As in "The Fire and the Hearth" Faulkner figures the death of his male protagonist's black mother at its most primitive level; that is how it felt to be suddenly and violently cut off or to cut oneself off from the black woman who had, as Edmonds says, "fed him from her own breast" (117).[45] Here Rider's body acts out the violence of his emptiness. Manny is not there to hold him, he can only hold himself. In one of the most powerful scenes of loss and mourning he ever wrote, Faulkner draws again upon his screen memory of being held by the quick, dark sister but still so terribly alone, kept aloof by the light of the white sister, the whiteness of racism.

The reason his community lynches Rider is because he breaks out of the myths invented to contain him. In doing so he creates his own myth, one which violates white culture's racial laws. He moves from wearing a mask of servility and deference to being a lawmaker. He remakes his public self as an avenging Old Testament God-figure and a black man who is deeply in love. Yet Rider is, first and foremost, like his inventor, a mythmaker. In effect, Faulkner is figuring as black both artistic marginalization and the passion which fuels art, or mythmaking. Its sources stream in part from an identification he can never acknowledge, which is why blackness in Faulkner's fictional world is freighted with such hatred and such desire.[46]

NOTES

1 Michael Millgate was among the first and remains the most reasoned and articulate proponent of this view. He begins his chapter on *Go Down, Moses* by noting that its publication "in May 1942 appears in retrospect as a moment of culmination in Faulkner's career. It marked the end of that supremely creative period which had begun with the writing of *The Sound and the Fury;* it was followed by six years of virtual silence during which Faulkner published only four short stories, none of them among his best." Noting that these were years Faulkner spent in Hollywood and

writing *A Fable*, he sees the author emerging "with the publication in 1948 of *Intruder in the Dust*, as apparently a different kind of novelist, much more ready to commit himself to specific statements on contemporary issues." *The Achievement of William Faulkner* (Lincoln: University of Nebraska Press, 1963), p. 201.

2 In *The Origins of Faulkner's Art* (Austin: University of Texas Press, 1984) I argued for the centrality of the Pierrot mask to Faulkner's imaginative apprenticeship – those ten years during which he wrote poetry almost exclusively. I also explained why he was drawn to that quintessential masker (whose venerable history begins in the Italian *Commedia dell'arte*), the favored persona of the symbolist and high modernist poets he then sought to emulate. Although I noted that the source of this figure's appeal was its protean and transgressive nature, my focus there was on how Faulkner the mediocre poet transformed himself into Faulkner the great novelist. Thus I only outlined some of the novelistic transformations to which Faulkner subjected his originary narrative voice. This essay, a section from the book I'm now completing, focuses almost exclusively on Faulkner's fiction – particularly *Go Down, Moses*. But my path into the intermingling of memory, desire, and race in Faulkner's fiction, as was Faulkner's, is through that persona from his poetic apprenticeship.

3 For such a reading see, for example, John Matthews' "The Ritual of Mourning in *Go Down, Moses*" in *The Play of Faulkner's Language* (Ithaca: Cornell University Press, 1982), pp. 212–273. Matthews notes that "the act of speaking griefs, which occupies all the stories, constitutes one of the unifying features of the novel" and argues persuasively that "Faulkner deliberately disfigures" the novel's structure "to show it buckling under the grief of the losses it sustains" (Matthews, 217). I agree that the novel is about loss, and find Matthews' reading thought provoking, but I am interested in Faulkner's subversive, personal, and therefore more coded figures of loss; how his own racial unconscious figures the threat of the loss of his artistic imagination which, for Faulkner, is the loss of Self.

4 "Screen memory" is the term Freud uses for early childhood memories which on their surface appear quite mundane, so mundane that it seems strange that they are so vividly remembered. Freud suggests that this discrepancy exists because "the relevant scene may perhaps have been incompletely retained in memory, and that may be why it seems so unenlightening." This occurs because the

forgotten though emotionally noteworthy experience has been repressed. Then, by means of condensation and displacement, the
conscious screen memory is created out of the material of the
repressed highly charged and unresolvable experience: "the parts
that have been forgotten probably contained everything that made
the experience noteworthy." What is remembered "is not the relevant experience itself" but *"another psychical element closely associated
with the objectionable one"* (my italics). That is, the conflict produced
by the original experience is responded to by a displacement of its
psychological meanings onto an indifferent image/memory. Calling
it indifferent is, in a sense, a kind of disguise. For example, Faulkner's screen memory concludes in what should be a moment of
relief – his aunts rescuing him and carrying him home. But as he
tells it, we can see that it's not a moment of relief at all. As soon as
one begins to translate a screen memory into language – to interpret it, to communicate it to someone else, as Faulkner did in this
letter – the so-called indifference falls away, revealing the essential
instability of the construction. Freud makes an analogy that is
useful here: "there is a common saying . . . about shams, that they
are not made of gold themselves, but have lain beside something
that *is* made of gold. The same simile might well be applied to some
of the experiences of childhood which have been retained in the
memory." He further notes that sometimes "screen memories will
. . . be formed from residues of memories relating to later life."
These "owe their importance to a connection with experiences in
early youth which have remained suppressed." Finally he suggests
that

[I]t may indeed be questioned whether we have any memories at all *from*
our childhood: memories *relating to* our childhood may be all that we
possess. Our childhood memories show us our earliest years not as they
were but as they appeared at later periods when these (early) memories
were (again) aroused. In these periods of arousal, the childhood memories
did not, as people are accustomed to say, emerge; they were formed at that
time. And a number of motives, with no concern for historical accuracy,
had a part in forming them, as well as in the selection of the memories
themselves. (Freud, "Screen Memories," 1899, *The Standard Edition,* 3, pp.
306–307, 320, 322)

See also "Introductory Lectures on Psychoanalysis" (1916), *The
Standard Edition,* 15, pp. 200–201.

In other words, it is impossible to date with any accuracy a screen
memory. If Faulkner's screen memory represents a condensation
and displacement of later racial knowledge, the memory suggests

that the earliest conflict he experienced was the tension produced by the demand on him to split his love between two mothers. This tension was later aggravated and racialized by his shame at knowing that the one who responded to and encouraged his own sensual responses and whom he apparently most desired was degraded and rendered taboo simply by the color of her skin. Thus his "loneliness and nameless sorrow" is for a desire that can never even be named, let alone satisfied. I would further question whether the fact that Faulkner had two early object-choices, both of whom were women, may have further complicated the oedipal anxieties of a young boy who experienced his alcoholic and emotionally distant father primarily as "lack." Faulkner's fascination with and remarkable insights concerning the permeability of his culture's racial and gender constructions suggests as much. (Many of these points were clarified for me in conversation with Harvey Strauss, M.D., President, Chicago Institute for Psychoanalysis.)

5 Joseph Blotner, ed., *Selected Letters of William Faulkner* (New York: Random House, 1977), p. 20, (hereafter SL).

6 I refer here to the most highly charged experiences of early development, those early issues that are, in Freud's sense, sexual.

7 *The Sound and the Fury* (New York: Vintage p.b., 1954). In Faulkner's fiction such figuring of blackness is not gender specific. For example, Temple Drake, Horace Benbow, and even Tommy the "feeb" experience Popeye, the white bootlegger and gangster "whose face had a queer bloodless color . . . a dead dark pallor," as black: "He smells black," Horace thinks, "like that black stuff that ran out of Bovary's mouth." Thus blackness translates as poison, suicide, and blood – the result of illicit desire. Identifying him with Emma Bovary, Horace feminizes and racializes Popeye – a typical rhetorical strategy for constructing an other. He also frames him with an iconic literary moment in a vain attempt to fictionalize and thus contain this man who mirrors him as he acts out Horace's own deepest fears and desires (*Sanctuary* [New York: Vintage p.b., 1993], p. 7. See also pp. 4, 5, 19, 42, 49, 67, 109, 121, 219, and passim).

8 Quentin, Mrs. Compson, and Jason all make this connection explicit in their derogatory racialized responses to either Caddy's or young Quentin's sexual behavior. Once Quentin determines that Caddy has "sinned" he projects his own fear of blackness onto her saying, *"Why wont you bring him to the house, Caddy? Why must you do like nigger women do in the pasture the ditches the dark woods hot hidden*

furious in the dark woods" but his language, echoing his memory/ fantasy of Natalie and himself in the hay, betrays his desire (SF, pp. 113–114). We know from the beginning of his monologue that Quentin believes that "a nigger is not a person so much as a form of behavior; a sort of obverse reflection of the white people he lives among" (SF, 106).

9   Faulkner rivets the reader's gaze on Rider's idealized and eroticized body: "the mounting sun sweat-glinted steel-blue on the midnight-colored bunch and slip of muscles" (144). Barr, as photographs show, was very dark. Faulkner's daughter elaborates: "When I'd ask her to tell me about her childhood, she'd distract me by saying, 'My Daddy was a lion, my Moma was a tigah, but people all say I'm an old Guinea Niggah.' Sometimes she'd say instead, a 'blue-gum niggah.' She had a relative called Aunt Blue-Gum who used to come to visit sometimes" (Jill Faulkner Summers, interview, 2 May 1989). Earlier I have argued that while Faulkner retained throughout his novelistic career the essential conception of sequence form developed during his years as a poet – elaborating on and embellishing it in his novels – he discarded the persona of Pierrot, while using his image as a source for character. See *Origins*. Thus in his novels he transforms – splits, multiplies, and disguises – the figure who dominates his poetry. Because my earlier book was essentially devoid of racial analysis, I missed Pierrot's reconstitution here as the artist's mask, at the moment when Faulkner has lost his black "mother."

10   Murry C. Falkner, *The Falkners of Mississippi* (Baton Rouge: Louisiana State University Press, 1967), p. 13 (hereafter TFM).

11   Malcolm Franklin, *Bitterweeds: Life with William Faulkner at Rowan Oak* (Irving, Texas: The Society for the Study of Traditional Culture, 1977), p. 110, and Jill Faulkner Summers, interview, 16 May 1983. This is confirmed by the daughter of Earl Wortham, the African-American blacksmith who cared for the Faulkners' horses. He and his wife were friends of Caroline Barr who often walked over to their home to visit with them:

"She was not off 'cause I don't think she had any days off. She would come like, you know back there the maids would fix breakfast and dinner and when she got through with all the dinner dishes on a day maybe when she didn't have to wash, she'd walk out to our house and eat with us and then she'd set there and chat awhile. Then she would walk back to her job. It would be time for her to prepare supper then. That's the way they did in those days. I think she had a little house somewhere on the place."

Evelyn Wortham Goliday says, "my father, who had known her

most of his life – he was just a boy under her – and his father had also worked for the Falkners, always told us that she came here *with* the Falkners. She raised them. She raised all the Faulkner children" (Pat Tingle, Research Assistant, interview with Evelyn Wortham Goliday, 8 March 1989). Although John Falkner, who was just under a year old when the Falkners left Ripley, and Joseph Blotner (quoting him) say Caroline Barr began working for the Falkners in 1907, five years after they moved to Oxford, William Faulkner's screen memory suggests that Malcolm Franklin and Faulkner's daughter are correct.

12   Summers, interview, 16 May 1983.

13   Summers, interview, 20 August 1980.

14   Summers, interviews, 23 February and 16 October 1987.

15   See p. 103, and Summers' interviews.

16   TFM, p. 13.

17   TFM, p. 15, and John Faulkner, *My Brother Bill: An Affectionate Reminiscence* (New York: Trident Press, 1963), pp. 48–49.

18   We never hear how *Henry* is damaged although perhaps we hear Faulkner's fervent wish when Henry refuses to share the same table with Carothers and he realizes "it was too late." Projecting his own shame onto his "brother" Carothers lashes out,

> "Are you ashamed to eat when I eat?" he cried.
> Henry paused, turning his head a little to speak in the voice slow and without heat: "I aint shamed of nobody," he said peacefully. "Not even me." (113–114)

19   WF to Robert K. Haas, 5 February 1940. Joseph Blotner, SL, p. 117.

20   By public and private discourse I mean to differentiate between the speech of facticity and his avowedly fictional texts, that is, between what he is reported to have said or what he wrote in essays, speeches, and letters or other "nonfictional" texts and what he wrote in his poetry, short stories, and novels.

21   Blotner, *Faulkner, A Biography* (New York: Random House, 1974) (hereafter FB), p. 1038 and SL, WF to Robert Haas, 7 February 1940, p. 118.

22   Blotner, FB, pp. 1034–1036 and SL, WF to Robert Haas, 7 February 1940, pp. 118–119.

23   Critics have written eloquently about Faulkner's fictional representations of these paradoxes and contradictions. Among the most interesting readings are Thadious Davis's *Faulkner's "Negro": Art and the Southern Context* (Baton Rouge: Louisiana State University Press, 1983), Minrose Gwin's chapter on *Absalom, Absalom!* in *Black and White Women of the Old South: The Peculiar Sisterhood in American*

Literature (Knoxville: University of Tennessee Press, 1985) and *The Feminine and Faulkner: Reading (Beyond) Sexual Difference* (Knoxville: University of Tennessee Press, 1990), and Diane Roberts' *Faulkner and Southern Womanhood* (Athens: University of Georgia Press, 1994).

24 Eric Lott's essays, " 'The Seeming Counterfeit': Racial Politics and Early Blackface Minstrelsy," *American Quarterly* 43.2 (June, 1991):223–254 and *"White Like Me:* Racial Cross-Dressing and the Construction of American Whiteness," in *United States Cultures of Imperialism,* eds. Amy Kaplan and Donald E. Pease (Duke, 1993), led me to realize that Faulkner's earliest and most enduring narrative consciousness, Pierrot in all his permutations, was perhaps the site from which to begin to study the contradictions in the racial consciousness tearing at the seams of *Go Down, Moses* by trying to answer the question I'd been ignoring for years: Why is Pantaloon/Pierrot here and why is he black?

25 When I first raised these issues at a Faulkner conference in Oxford, Mississippi, in August 1987, I drew many deeply felt and thoughtful responses. I include one of those here not only because it is representative, but also because it is among the most articulate and sensitive and, all unconsciously, makes precisely the same point:

[A]s regards the question you raised about how Callie Barr's attitudes about and experiences with men might have influenced Faulkner's. I suspect that you will find that they were minimal, given the whole Southern social system.

Let me share my experience, which is probably characteristically Southern. My mother died a few days after my birth and my brother and I were raised by a Black mammy for four years, until my father remarried. Afterwards, she continued to work for the family for the next 25 years until her retirement. After that I continued to take care of her, to regard her emotionally as a mother surrogate, and when she died I overruled my family's resistance and buried her in my cemetery plot. But in spite of that lifetime of emotional closeness, I never regarded her attitudes about men and marriage or religion as anything other than particular and peculiar to her own culture. I suppose some equivalent for a Northern family would be, say, a Lutheran family with a Catholic nanny. In spite of their closeness on a personal level, they would regard her attitudes about church, sexuality, sin, politics, or marriage as exotic. So I doubt you will find Callie Barr's perceptions ultimately threw much weight with Faulkner. (Thorton F. Jordon, Columbus, Georgia, in a letter to the author, 9 August 1987)

26 "The Integration of Faulkner's *Go Down, Moses,*" *Critical Inquiry* 12.2 (Winter, 1986), p. 423.

27 William Faulkner, *Go Down, Moses* (New York: Vintage p.b., 1973), p. 135. *The Jazz Singer,* the movie in which its star, Al Jolson, in

blackface, sings his famous rendition of "Mammy," was first released in 1927. Michael North notes the "prevalence of blackface routines in film, onstage, and even on radio." For example, 1927 also saw the release of *Uncle Tom's Cabin,* D. W. Griffith's comic version of the same story, and blackface films starring Eddie Cantor and W. C. Fields. See North, *The Dialect of Modernism: Race, Language, and Twentieth Century Literature* (New York: Oxford University Press, 1994), pp. 4–8, 197–198, n. 6–7.

28 "Change the Joke and Slip the Yoke" in *Shadow and Act* (New York: Random House, 1964), pp. 49, 53.

29 Two others were "The Old People," which Faulkner had sent to his agent, Harold Ober, on October 3, 1939, and "The Fire and the Hearth," which he had sent along with "Pantaloon." SL, WF to Robert K. Haas, Wednesday, 22 May 1940, p. 124.

30 SL, WF to RH, 28 April 1940, p. 122.

31 SL, p. 125. In an attempt to get his publisher to raise his fees, he also began negotiations with a new publisher which left him only the time and energy, he wrote, to write "trash" (SL, p.121). By the end of July the negotiations had fallen through and Faulkner again wrote Random House about *Go Down, Moses,* saying that he needed to write one more story, "a novella, actually" to complete the book but that he'd have to write a book he could sell fast first (more "trash") as he didn't want the novella published separately. SL, p. 135.

32 Blotner, *Faulkner, A Biography,* One Volume Edition (New York: Random House, 1984), p. 424, and Tom Dardis, *The Thirsty Muse: Alcohol and the American Writer* (New York: Ticknor and Fields, 1989), p. 70. Dardis's chapter on Faulkner is an intelligent and forthright discussion of the author's progressively serious alcoholism and its relation to his writing. Dardis documents Faulkner's addiction as already beyond control by January 1936 (Dardis, 26).

33 For further instances in which alcohol is reified see also pp. 205, 226, 228, 249, 251, and 310.

34 Faulkner to Haas, 1 May 1941, SL, pp. 139–141.

35 Faulkner took his book dedication from Barr's eulogy, which he read at the service he conducted at Rowan Oak prior to the Negro Baptist Church services (Blotner 1974, 1035–1036).

36 It occurs to me that these constrictions are also the dungeon which Quentin Compson describes so eloquently as that "dark place into which a single weak ray of light came slanting upon two faces lifted out of the shadow. . . . the dungeon was Mother herself she and

Father upward into weak light holding hands and us lost some-where below even them without even a ray of light" (SF 215).

37 WF in letter to Robert Haas, 7 February 1940, SL 118–119.

38 Patricia Tingle (Research Assistant), interview with Rachel Mc Geehee, Caroline Barr's niece (and Mc Geehee's daughter Mildred Quarles), 16 February 1989.

39 Patricia Tingle (Research Assistant), interview with Mildred Quarles, 29 March 1989.

40 North, *Dialect of Modernism*. See pp. 5–8 for his discussion of this film.

41 Eric Lott, *Love and Theft: Blackface Minstrelsy and the American Working Class* (New York: Oxford University Press, 1993), pp. 188, 189.

42 I have developed this point in *Origins*. See especially pp. 129–151 for a discussion of the composite Pierrot of Faulkner's poetic apprenticeship, the persona who informs "Pantaloon." In *Origins* I just note similarities in some core images that compose these poetic Pierrot figures' psychic worlds. The silver moonlight (of racism) frames and encloses Rider and his hound as does the drunk (bad/black?) Pierrot's white "foster mother," the moon who "weaves moon-madness" in his head and who looks "like a dismembered breast" (142, 148; William Faulkner, *The Marionettes* [Charlottes-ville: The University Press of Virginia, 1977], pp. 15, 17, 6). Rider, like the Pierrot of *Vision in Spring* "spins and whirls," in a commu-nity that does not speak his language. *Vision's* Pierrot, the poet who is afraid to speak, sits "alone" "small and high on a mountain top" in "a cage of moonlight" (Austin: University of Texas Press, 1984), pp. 10, 11, 18. His moon "is a spider on the sky/ Weaving her icy silver across his heart" and freezing him into a blue and silver column against which "the air icily splinters and glistens." In the moonlight of "Pantaloon" "moonshine" transforms Rider as the silver air – the bootleg whiskey he drinks to dull his grief – congeals in his throat and three times "sprang" from his mouth in "a solid and unmoving column, . . . columnar and intact . . . outward glint-ing in the moonlight, splintering, vanishing . . . silvering, glinting, shivering" (149).

43 Here too, as in many other American fictions besides Faulkner's, miscegenation is figured as incest, thus racializing the oedipal con-flict.

44 The resonance here between Rider and Joe Christmas, perhaps Faulkner's most racially and sexually irresolute protagonist, is con-

scious and deliberate. Faulkner's readers are meant to hear and explore its aesthetic, personal, and political meanings.

45 Carothers Edmonds mystifies racism, thus implicitly denying responsibility for his actions, by calling it "the old curse of his fathers" (111). But after he becomes a racist, his foster mother Molly Beauchamp shocks the boy – to the enormity of *his* loss – by refusing to let him eat with her family: "The table was set in the kitchen where it always was . . . but . . . there was just one chair, one plate, his glass of milk beside it, the platter heaped with untouched chicken, and even as he sprang back, gasping, for an instant blind as the room rushed and swam, Henry was turning toward the door to go out of it" (113). The enormity of his aloneness and the violence of his resulting fear and rage at the emptiness he feels are imaged here, as they will be in "Pantaloon," as food made by the black mother/lover but no longer shared with her. Put simply, the breast denied. Edmonds speaks with his body as does Rider because in their rage they regress to the presymbolic.

46 Faulkner first codes artistic marginalization as black in his second novel. In the first instance, an eighteen-year-old naif who immediately recognizes the sculptor Gordon's genius asks, "Why are you so black?" He repeats the color and she responds, " 'Not your hair and beard. I like your red hair and beard. But you. You are black. I mean . . . ' her voice fell and he suggested Soul? 'I don't know what that is,' she stated quietly" (Faulkner, *Mosquitoes* [New York: Laurel p.b. 1955], p. 22). This becomes even more explicit in the following exchange between Jenny and Pat. Jenny says,

"I got to talking to a funny man. A little kind of black man – "

"A nigger?"

"No. He was a white man, except he was awful sunburned and kind of shabby dressed – no necktie and hat. Say, he said some funny things to me. . . . He said he was a liar by profession, and he made good money at it, enough to own a Ford as soon as he got it paid out. I think he was crazy. Not dangerous: just crazy . . . . [His name was] Faulkner." (*Mosquitoes*, 119–120)

6

The Game of Courts: *Go Down, Moses,* Arbitrary Legalities, and Compensatory Boundaries

THADIOUS M. DAVIS

> The control the court sought was the *total* submission of blacks.
> A. Leon Higginbotham, Jr., *In the Matter of Color: Race and the American Legal Process: The Colonial Period,* p. 9.

> In trying to describe the provisional aspect of slave law, I would choose words that revealed its structure as rooted in a concept of ... black antiwill. I would characterize the treatment of blacks by whites in their law as defining blacks as those who had no will. ... if "pure will" or total control equals the perfect white person, then, impure will and total lack of control equals the perfect black person.
> Patricia J. Williams, *The Alchemy of Race and Rights: Diary of a Law Professor,* p. 219.

The Game of Genre

Masculinist sport and games are interconnected with property and law in representing racialized society in *Go Down, Moses.* In the social state of Faulkner's text, sport and games derive meanings from an effort to duplicate the competition for and control of property within the circumscription of law. Both law and games are forms of social control and discursive bodies of social commentary. Legal boundaries are, however, all arbitrary, but also compensatory for players whose moves are regulated by rules displaced or dislodged from the assumptions of law within the social state. These seemingly disparate modes of thinking about the text contribute to an interpretive strategy for reading *Go Down, Moses* – one that allows for the multivocality and density of ideas (both compatible and competing ideas) in Faulkner's text. In reading the white masculinist power dynamics of law and property combined with games and sport, I consider the condition of enslavement and domination, the difference of race and of gender, and the naturalizing of change and instability.[1] The tenuous connections of game, play, and sport to the text come together momentarily in this reading of two competing narratives: a narrative of legality with property and ownership at its core; a narrative of games with masculinist sport and social ritual at its center.

I am not attempting to insert a new metanarrative into the criticism or to uncover a new master narrative within the text, but rather to intervene in already existing determinations of the hermetic, coherent, stable text; and to expand its reading as multiply interpretable. Despite the many possible readings that justify exclusive claims of its organic unity, *Go Down, Moses* reasserts itself as problematic in terms of conventional definitions of genre. The question of whether *Go Down, Moses* is a novel or a story sequence has been situated at the center of readings of Faulkner's text, but I believe that the question of genre for *Go Down, Moses* does not have to be answered in either-or/neither-nor terms. If claims of unity are dissolved by the reader self-authorized to create a reading experience out of engagement with the text, and if claims of fragmentation (that is, story sequence) are suspended by the configuration of games marking the text as both contest and contested site, then momentarily at least Faulkner's authority over his text becomes bounded and the issue of its genre transgressable. Accordingly, I locate Tomey's Turl, rather than Isaac McCaslin or his ancestor Lucius Quintus Carothers McCaslin, as a figure of transgression and hybridity at the center of this project. His given name is Terrel, but that he is most often called Tomey's Turl seems appropriate because that name retains his social history, positions him outside of McCaslin domination, and refigures his mother who died giving birth to him. His genesis is bodily in a game of running that culminates in a game of hide-and-seek; materially in an enactment of property ownership; and textually in a word game that is transcribed in a legal record.

Born in slavery during June of 1833, *"yr stars fell,"* Tomey's Turl is the son of Tomasina and the grandson of Eunice.[2] Because his enslavement follows from the condition of his mother, Tomey's Turl is, like his mother and grandmother, the property of Carothers McCaslin. In the 1780s, Lucius Quintus Carothers McCaslin left Carolina with his slaves; in Mississippi he purchased land from a Chickasaw and created a plantation.[3] Tomey's Turl is both the son and the grandson of Carothers McCaslin, who violates his own daughter Tomasina and fathers her son. Tomey's Turl's textualized origin appears to be a word game analogous to the Sphinx's riddle that Oedipus solves. His lineage is embedded in the "facts" recorded riddlelike in the McCaslin commissary ledgers and "decoded" by another grandson of Carothers McCaslin, Ike McCaslin, who functions as detective solving a crime puzzle and as reader creating meaning in a fashion similar to that of Quentin Compson in *Absalom, Absalom!* The encoded incest committed by Carothers and revealed by Ike has most typically led to a focus on the white McCaslin men (e.g., their relation to the land and to slavery, their exercise of power or repudiation of it, their subjugation of blacks and women) as a way of reading identity, familial or cultural formation, and disintegration in the text. Rarely has it resulted in considering the text as a configuration of Tomey's Turl's hybridity or of his position as a figure of transgression against the political economy and social order dominating the text. The games that mark *Go Down, Moses* as contest and contested site also mark Tomey's Turl as the trope, the embodiment, the represented contest and contested site, that necessarily refocus attention to the text.

In refusing to locate a reading of the text in an already identified or a possibly identifiable master code, I am also refusing to accept the "right" of a master's authority over slave, over property, and ultimately over historical and cultural forces as signifiers. I am remembering the point made by A. Leon Higginbotham, when he remarked "a nexus between the brutal centuries of colonial slavery and the racial polarization and anxieties of today. The poisonous legacy of legalized oppression based upon the matter of color can never be adequately purged from our society if we act as if slave laws never existed."[4] I am asserting, too, that Tomey's Turl should not be "unrighted," because as Patricia Williams has observed in an essay entitled "On Being the Object of Property," "In law, rights are islands of empowerment.

To be unrighted is to be disempowered, and the line between rights and no-rights is most often the line between dominators and oppressors."[5] The legal language of rights becomes a reminder of the possibility of imaginary empowerment. "Rights contain images of power," Williams has said, "and manipulating those images, either visually or linguistically, is central in the making and maintenance of rights. In principle, therefore, the more dizzyingly diverse the images that are propagated, the more empowered we will be in society" (Williams 234). Her statements set off the sparks that enabled my project here and allowed me to rethink *Go Down, Moses* with Tomey's Turl at the center.

Thus, for me as a racially defined woman reading reflexively, the text can be situated in terms of political action, of the assertion of civil rights, and of resistance to the domination of ideological tyrants. The historical conditions of western expansion (the settling of the Mississippi frontier) and of chattel slavery (the establishing of legal slavery), I consider inscriptions of a white masculinist consolidation of power in property and pleasure in progeny (without the intermediate stage of sexual intercourse which is always already over in the construction of this text and which may be read as rape in the case of Carothers McCaslin's sexual aggression against Tomasina). In the struggle for consolidations of power is the seldom visible resistance to subjugation and the rarely articulated countermove for empowerment. The text's historical engagements foreground, then, the social and legal contests for power that motivate positioning Tomey's Turl both as a "righted" challenge to domination and as a "willful" site of resistance to oppression.

The Game of Challenge

"A game is a description of strategic interaction that includes the constraints on the actions that the players *can* take and the players' interests, but does not specify the actions that the players *do* take."[6] Tomey's Turl is initially constructed in the ambiguity of relational identity, and in the context of an unclarified species of runaway: " 'Damn the fox,' Uncle Buck said. 'Tomey's Turl has broke out again' " (5). Tomey's Turl is also constituted as a game player, however, using games as a site of resistance to power. The dialectic between his social condition (as a slave who has run) and his individual autonomy (as the instigator of a game in which he is a major and decisive player) produces his identity. He is represented as a rational decision maker who pursues a defined objective, and who strategizes on the basis of his knowledge of how the other players will behave: "he went there every time he could slip off, which was about twice a year. He was heading for Mr Hubert Beauchamp's place. . . . Tomey's Turl would go there to hang around Mr Hubert's girl, Tennie, until sombody came and got him" (5). Tomey's Turl is represented in motion, in action, and thus as an agent, even though his agency is constrained by two sets of circumstances: the racist ideology informing the conceptions of "nigger" and enslaved property; and the game strategy of silence that disallows his voicing either the motive or the desire in his behavior.

Beginning with Tomey's Turl's running, *Go Down, Moses* deploys games (fox hunting with dogs, gambling with cards and dice, racing) as constructions both of chance and of strategy which represent the arbitrariness and the boundedness of forms of identity, and economic and social interaction as these forms intersect with the regularity, protection, and compensation of law. "Social interaction appears to reproduce unceasingly an interplay of differing preferences within which individuals run the risk of upsetting society by following their egotistical impulses. Rational understanding of this conflict of interest leads to what game theory terms a game of strategy."[7] Games of strategy are different from games of skill and chance, because they require the player to assume a role, which he conceives and acts out. The assumption of the role of player within the game becomes a form of social empowerment, even though it may conflict with accepted social beliefs or codes. Laws are, like games, manifestations of social practices. "Law represents both a discourse and a process of power. Norms created by and enshrined in law are manifestations of power relations. These norms are coercively applied and justified in part by the perception that they are 'neutral' and 'objective.' "[8]

The legal codes constricting Tomey's Turl to a nonrelational positionality in regard to the McCaslin twins, Theophilus (Buck) and Amodeus (Buddy), are those that define a slave as property and as labor, not as human or as brother. Slave law rests on the motivating principle of "undifferentiated communalism," which reduces all slaves to labor under the total social control of masters who own labor.[9] This principle of slave law is not merely a matter of economic exploitation of "labor"; it is an ultimate formulation of dehumanization, of negating the human being and treating that negated "thing" as an abstraction termed "labor." That Tomey's Turl is constructed visually as "that damn white half-McCaslin" (6), positions him on the boundary of race and slave law.

Because the laws of society are suspended in play, sport, and games, and replaced by a new order of rules and regulations, games provide freedom from the normal social order and its dehumanizing boundaries in *Go Down, Moses*. In this context, Tomey's Turl attains freedom within the "free space" games represent. Despite the imposition of another formulaic set of boundaries within the duration of a game, games are attractive precisely because of their freedom from the restrictions of society and from the power hierarchy controlling racial interaction. Games clear a neutral space for the reformation of the possibilities of interaction based on the terms and conditions of the game. In Tomey's Turl's case, he resists confinement within the ideologies of race by reordering his world and reconstituting himself as empowered to act and to be a subject. He intervenes in the legal practice of dehumanization and reclassifies himself against the hegemonic ideology and structure of a slave culture.

Within his game of "runaway," Tomey's Turl assumes subjectivity. He is active, he is intentional, and he is inquiring. He can negotiate the alternative strategizing of his would-be captors, Buck McCaslin and his nephew Cass Edmonds, who are also his opponent game players, convinced that he is beatable in the race to the Beauchamp place, because "nobody had ever known Tomey's Turl to go faster than his natural walk, even riding a mule" (8). The game Tomey's Turl initiates is variously labeled a run (race), a hunt, a chase, a contest, and a courtship. It can be defined, however, as a game of challenge and a stratagem for exercising will. It functions within the formal characteristics of play as "a free activity standing quite consciously outside 'ordinary' life" and "proceed[ing] within its own proper boundaries of time and space according to fixed rules and in an orderly manner."[10] As a "stepping out of 'real' life into a temporary sphere of activity with a disposition of its own," Tomey's Turl's game "is 'played out' within certain limits of time and place" and "contains its own course and meaning" (Huizinga 26, 28). In general, his moves challenge the power and authority of whites over him. In particular, his moves challenge one key aspect of his containment in slavery: his right to sexual expression which has been excluded from the eccentric world of the McCaslin place. He challenges the right of his McCaslin owners to restrict his courtship of Tennie, to deny his desire for a wife, or to enforce conformity to their refusal of sexuality.

Read from the perspective of Tomey's Turl as a race for full expression of a mature, sexual self within society, the game of runaway is a periodic reminder that despite attempts to reduce slaves to children without will, enslavement did not necessarily produce simplistic objects of property. Tomey's Turl's game of challenge takes on the cultural logic and hegemony based on the legal conception of "black antiwill" that would determine his total subjugation in a social, economic, and political order. Master-slave relations function unlike market theory which "always takes attention away from the full range of human potential in its pursuit of a divinely willed, rationally inspired, invisibly handed economic actor"; as Patricia Williams reminds us, "Master-slave relations took attention away from the full range of black human potential in a somewhat different way: it pursued a vision of blacks as simple-minded, strong-bodied economic 'actants' " (Williams 220).

Unlike Buck and, in particular, Buddy, Tomey's Turl is not content to remain in an unattached social condition. In desiring a mate and in specifying the mate he desires, he separates himself from the undifferentiated middle-aged "boys" at the McCaslin place. Buck and Buddy are, in Daniel Hoffman's view, "superannuated boys," who "turn all of life into games."[11] Buck and Buddy are constructed within the social roles designated as masculine and feminine, but they play off the expectations for gender formation within their society. Buck drinks, wears a tie, farms the land, and socializes outside the confines of his property; Buddy cooks, does not drink, and remains at home in an unconventional domestic space (he is, nevertheless, the expert poker player). Buck resists courting Sophonsiba Beauchamp because the twins exist within a space where "ladies were so damn seldom thank God that a man could ride for days in a straight line without having to dodge a single one" (7), and within that space they can behave without acknowledging their sexuality, or the misogyny implicated in their descriptions of women.

Like Buck and Buddy, Tomey's Turl does not escape the cultural formation of roles. He is labeled "nigger" (9, 10), and objectified outside of the expected code of behavior of (white) men, whose racialization is assumed: "Because, being a nigger, Tomey's Turl should have jumped down and run for it afoot as soon as he saw them. But he didn't; maybe Tomey's Turl had been running off from Uncle Buck for so long that he had even got used to running away like a white man would do it" (8–9). The boundary of race is an already existing social condition in the games on which the narrative depends, in the binary oppositional of freedom, and in the social interactions among the players. The frequency with which Buck refers to Tomey's Turl as "my nigger" fixes his racialization within the economy of slavery and establishes his subordination to his owner's legal authority over him. (It also routinizes both the epithet and the racist hierarchy.) Despite the ridicule heaped upon his racialized body and upon his determined efforts to be with Tennie, Tomey's Turl is differentiated from the twins in the process of rejecting the label "boy" and of coming into a (sexual) maturity as a man.

Courtship is a crucial aspect of Tomey's Turl's maturation. His courtship of Tennie is methodical and directed. Twice a year, he heads for her cabin on the Beauchamp plantation although he knows their enslavement represents an impasse, a stalemate, because neither of their owners will relinquish their property to a marriage. His tactic is not merely recursive, it also allows for the development of responses to his repeated actions; for example, Buck can court Sophonsiba Beauchamp as a result of, and in response to, Tomey's Turl's running. By repeating his game of running to court Tennie, Tomey's Turl redefines the social life of the McCaslins to include interdependence and interaction, which open the potential for their understanding that social life is also "about display, confrontation, exhibition and questions of tolerance."[12] Buck's reluctant courtship is an indirect and evasive tactical game that functions in cooperation with Tomey's Turl's strategically repeated game.[13] In negotiating that courtship as "protection" (12) of his own, Tomey's Turl impacts upon his future and on that of his white owners whose authority over him is legally complete.

The narrative privileges Buck's donning a tie before chasing Tomey's Turl as a sign of his intention to court Sophonsiba, but it obscures the detail that Tomey's Turl dons his white Sunday shirt before beginning his run. In this act of dressing up, of dressing "white," of transforming himself into a "gentleman," Turl announces that different rules are in motion from those that obtain while he remains on the McCaslin place. Buck undergoes a similar process when he puts on the tie. In playing out another existence through clothing as a disguise, both Tomey's Turl and Buck become different men and act outside their typical social and cultural realities. In producing an image of himself that is different from his everyday asexual, subjugated self, Tomey's Turl suspends the boundaries and codes of that life. Concomitantly, he instigates the ritual that forces Buck to do the same: "The only time he wore the necktie was on Tomey's Turl's account" (7). And, therefore, Buck allows himself to become "suitor" and Sophonsiba Beauchamp to become the object of his sexual interest and offhanded courtship.

The behavior of the player-characters (Buck, Buddy, Hubert, and Tomey's Turl) is predictable, based upon what they have to win or lose in acting in a particular way. Moves and countermoves in *Go Down, Moses* are much like the strategy of the game of chess in *Light in August* (1932), and like the game of stalking that Charles Bon initiates in *Absalom, Absalom!* (1936), or the game of one-upmanship played by Thomas Sutpen in the same novel as he maneuvers to build his dynasty and plantation.[14] Starting with Freud's 1913 mention of chess, that game has been viewed psychoanalytically as a reenactment of the oedipal conflict, with the (unconscious) goal of patricide manifested as "checkmate," trapping the king. More recently, however, psychologist Reuben Fine has observed that chess involves a sublimation of homosexual impulses; moreover, chess has been described as a competitive sport of mental aggression in which the objective is to defeat the opponent's intellect or to crush someone's ego.[15] Although the strategies of chess as a contest of will, intellect, and memory, with already established and defined sequences of potential moves but with the added complexity of insolubility, inform the predictability of moves by characters in *Go Down, Moses,* Tomey's Turl's action and proclivity for playing well, for regulating his own moves skillfully, and for anticipating the moves of his opponents in the woods, all prefigure Isaac McCaslin and his mentor Sam Fathers, who in "The Old People" and "The Bear" are drawn to rituals of the woods, the hunt and the society of hunters and who accept the boundaries and the freedoms imposed by the code of hunting. Hunting is a form of cultural play throughout *Go Down, Moses;* as a cultural phenomenon, it allows for male hunters as signifiers of society to express their interpretation of life and the world.[16]

The main narrative of "Was" begins with a parodied hunt, a wild chase of a fox by a pack of dogs (4–5). That chase is contained within the McCaslin house and inscribed as a "good race," though it is obviously comedic and parodistic.[17] When viewed as sport or play, this kind of hunting – fox hunting – emphasizes a leisure-class activity which both adheres to and dismisses everyday societal rules, but this particular interior-bound fox hunt and the incidents that follow resist the expected cultural symbolic. Tomey's Turl assumes the object position and the symbolic determinants of the fox in the chase, and though he similarly runs within a confined and defined area, he is running away from his own enslavement by his owners, the McCaslin twins. "The contract between play and seriousness is always fluid," because the "inferiority of play is continually being offset by the corresponding superiority of its seriousness" (*Homo Ludens,* 27). The parodistic play of "Was" extends to the title, which, as Daniel Hoffman notices, Faulkner uses despite saying: "There is no such thing as *was* – only *is*. If *was* existed, there would be no grief or sorrow."[18] The "was" that exists in this text thus constitutes a lack of "grief" and "sorrow," emotions replaced by a naively utopian vision of the challenge to authority and containment as necessarily victorious and good natured. The privileging of humor, however, at the expense of the characters racialized as black promotes and maintains racist cultural stereotyping, which reverberates throughout the remainder of *Go Down, Moses*, troubling thereafter both the constructions of race and the production of textual coherence. It is a cruel extension of the destabilization of black identity and subjectivity explicit in slave law and in slavery (ownership of blacks as property without will) and in Tomey's Turl's birth (death of his mother and his grandmother and rejection by his father). The farcical, cruel sleight of hand in "Was" proceeds uninterrogated in the narrative and is a signification of Faulkner's problematical game of genre.

Tomey's Turl as a runaway represents the fluidity of boundaries both in "real" life and in "make believe" or play. Although the absurdity of a fox hunt in a house is underscored by the absurdity of "the dogs' room" inside that house, the relation between the house and family remains unmarked so that the absurdity of a hunt within a space defined as family for a member of the family goes without commentary. No matter how broad their comic gestures or unorthodox their living arrangements, Buck and Buddy naturalize racial distinctions, racial hierarchies, and racial power. The silence in the text that is not immediately perceived has to do with the relationship between the white men and the black object of their hunt. Although family slaves were held to be "special" under slave law, slaves without such connections were ruled on differently: "No sacrifice of feeling, no consideration of humanity, are involved. These were not family slaves, but strangers . . . casually purchased at a public sale; no statement that they were peculiarly valuable for their character, qualities, or skill in any trade or handicraft."[19] Although Tomey's Turl may receive "special" consideration because of his public "identity" as a family slave (and thus as having ties of sentiment), he receives none as a family member. That concealed and suppressed identification is disallowed under the law, and thus rendered invisible and nonexistent.

Implicitly, law functions in the same space as the card game, which becomes a contest for possession of blacks and women – for blacks in the legal bondage of slavery and for women in the legal institution of marriage. Unlike the game of running invented by Tomey's Turl out of a cruel necessity, the games of chance and sport are not only gendered masculine but racialized "white," because they are a means of maintaining hegemony and of exerting social control. Their outcomes directly impact upon women and blacks, as in the fate of women – both the white Sophonsiba and the black Tennie – and of Tomey's Turl. In the two poker games between first Buck and then Buddy McCaslin and Hubert Beauchamp, the intersection of laws and games occurs. The wagers reflect the "undifferentiated individualism" that Mark Tushnet has identified as the motivating principle of bourgeois law which

embodies a strong presumption that all transactions involve completely fungible commodities. Thus, where some transaction goes awry, the law presumes that things can be set straight by a monetary award of appropriate damages, for the parties are presumed to be unconcerned about the transaction itself so long as they receive the profits, whether from the transaction or from some other source. (Tushnet 157–159)

But the confusion of the bet – the slippage between money ($500 and $300), slave property (Tomey's Turl and Tennie), and white female relative (Sophonsiba Beauchamp) – occurs because slaves are not "completely fungible commodities." It is, for example, Tomey's Turl who deals the hand in the poker game and imposes his will upon the outcome.

Because within the institution of slavery, one slave is interchangeable for another, because a slave is defined as "labor" rather than as "laborer," when Hubert Beauchamp calls for "the first creature that answers, animal mule or human, that can deal ten cards" (25), he thus predictably does not notice that Tomey's Turl responds to the call. Tomey's Turl's desperate gambit succeeds. His strategic location as dealer signifies a challenge to the social order and its arbitrary codes. The hand of stud poker he deals for Hubert Beauchamp and Buddy McCaslin renders relative the "rules" of the game and its stated objective. His move outwits Beauchamp as an opponent who would neither buy Tomey's Turl so that he could marry Tennie nor have "that damn white half-McCaslin on his place even as a free gift" (6). Tomey's Turl's move places him in collusion with Buddy, who in his position as twin to Buck had been committed to capturing the runaway.

The winning of the hand, however, is a white man's game. Tomey's Turl returns to enslavement within the McCaslin land and as McCaslin property, but with a difference. Not only does he return with the woman he has courted, Tennie, who will become his wife, but also he returns marked as an adult. The game has been a rite of passage and of personhood (marriage as the province of the adult, fully matured body). Nevertheless, because emancipation is not the objective of his run, he cannot facilitate social reconstruction. The imaginary is decidedly white, male, and patriarchal. Tomey's Turl's "win," because it is mediated through the "win" of the white slaveholding Buddy as a superior card player, does not constitute an abolitionist blow to the institution of slavery.

The poker game of "Was" is related to the crap games in "Pantaloon in Black," in which Rider as a gambling man and a black, violates not the rules of a dice game, but of the social configurations governing the interactions of black and white men. Rider, whose remarkable physical strength and agility signify his athleticism, can be read as a runaway from the material reality of his life after his wife's death, and as a game player attempting to cross the physical barrier between death and life actuated by his experiential reality as a game player. His renewed courtship of Mannie after her death involves him in a form of athletic play with rules of its own, as is suggested when he shovels dirt into Mannie's grave with a shovel that in his hands "resembled the toy shovel a child plays with at the shore" (131). This reconfiguration of the adult Rider signals his out-of-the-ordinary state, in which he desires death. His "artistry of consciousness and bodily presence," to use Joseph Mihalich's term for the lived experience of sports and athletics, is bracketed by "spontaneity and inventiveness (without arbitrariness)" and signals his attunement with the experiential world; in this existential state, Rider as athlete "does not think about space and time in the world," he "lives space and time in the world in his . . . acute expression of consciousness-in-the-world-with-a-body."[20]

In contrast to the "mute click and scutter of the dice" (147), Rider gives voice to the cheating, and articulates the crimes committed against blacks even in games of chance (148), where cheating increases the arbitrary power over them. According to the uncomprehending sheriff's deputy, "the same crap game where Birdsong has been running crooked dice on them mill niggers for fifteen years, goes straight to the same game where he had been peacefully losing a probably steady average ninety-nine percent of his pay ever since he got big enough to read the spots on them miss-out dice" (151). That Birdsong had been cheating for a long time and that the players knew of the second set of dice up his sleeve would be appropriate conclusions to draw. These two pieces of information suggest that a different set of rules applied to this crap game based on its significant deviations from other crap games not routinized as crooked, and that this specific crap game images white-black power relations in the social world. Rider's response to the game is predicated upon both his anticipation of the outcome and upon his ancillary contest against containment. He resists accepting the "rules" of the game that signify the barriers preventing his reunion with his dead wife, and that very resistance defies the logic of race in his society. Rider's story thus achieves what Tomey's Turl's cannot: It names the misreading underlying racial stereotyping. In so doing, it doubly inscribes irony into the dissonance of the larger text.

The Object of Property

Tomey's Turl's identity is incomplete both in "Was" and in reading his subjectivity as game player. Tomey's Turl is owned. He is property, whose "rightful" owners Buck and Buddy McCaslin also happen to be his brothers, sons of the same father. Turl exercises his agency by running at will and by courting the woman of his choice, but he is represented neither as an autonomous being nor as a serious subject; this lack fractures any attempt to read *Go Down, Moses* as a unified, coherent project. His construction as visually "white" though he should be "black," and as relationally "half-McCaslin" when his father and mother are both McCaslins, argues for the slippage between discrete categories of race. Nonetheless, against the logic of experience, the categories are maintained by slavery as binary and impenetrable, and Tomey's Turl is racialized as black and abstracted as fatherless. Tomey's Turl is chattel, the enslaved black who can be denied paternity and thus fraternity. He is the object of property.

Property is an inscription of the hegemony of the male symbolic. In *Go Down, Moses,* questions about law and legality originate in the perspective of white male southerners (even when interpolated by black men, such as Lucas Beauchamp, Tomey's Turl's son), who possess, own, inherit, and hold "property," and whose right to dispose of it as they choose is protected by law. The total control of property assumed in the rights of ownership leads to domination and abuse. Property includes people of two classes: blacks and women, both of whom are objects of property and objectified as property under the laws of patriarchy and of slavery. Both blacks and women are abused and dominated under the expectations of male hegemonic configured as property. The social/familial discourse and the legal/cultural discourse both elucidate and collide to express the otherness of blacks and women, and to signal an incomplete but complicated effort to retain and restrain them in the position of other by means of justifying their different expressive codes.

In a discourse on law and property, Jeremy Bentham states: "That which in the natural state was an almost invisible thread, in the social state becomes a cable. Property and law are born together. Before laws were made there was no property; take away laws and property ceases. The organs of the law are symbiotic with property."[21] Property is, then, a legal construction. The arbitrariness of law is linked, in one respect, to its shaping originary existence in the protection of property and the rights of the property owner. Men who own property also control the boundaries of that property and production relations, and thus also control law and the legal discourses constructed to protect their holdings. "Law has developed over time in the context of theories and institutions which are controlled by men and reflect their concerns. Historically, law has been a 'public' arena and its focus has been on public concerns" (Fineman xiii). As a discourse of power expressive of the interests of men, law has not attended well to those traditionally controlled, defined, and silenced by "private recesses of society" (Fineman xiii); for example, blacks as the object of property and of slave law.

Riddlelike and echoing his complicated birth and ambiguous position within the household, Tomey's Turl's utterances are minimal and coded: " 'And nem you mind that neither. I got protection now. All I needs to do is to keep Old Buck from ketching me unto I gets the word' " (12). His enforced subordination demands silences, so that his private injuries cannot become the subject of legal or social appeals: " 'I gonter tell you something to remember: anytime you wants to get something done, from hoeing out a crop to getting married, just get the women-folks to working on it. Then all you needs to do is set down and wait. You member that' " (13). He remains fixed in an object position that does not allow him to negotiate meaning himself or to articulate his own meaning. The right to property (public/ social, ownership, and entitlement) necessarily competes with the right to subjectivity (privacy, "life, liberty, and the pursuit of happiness"). Tomey's Turl's oppression and exploitation are contingent on his being silent and verbally unintelligible as the object of property toward whom the exercise of discourses of legal authority and social power is complete.

Like Tomey's Turl, both black and white women in *Go Down, Moses* are located as the objects of property in a paternalistic system that would suppress their agency and, within legal constructions, determine their meaning. The difference between white and black women is slight, but significant: black women are not protected by the legal system but by the codes of conduct and the ideological formations within white patriarchal southern society. Eunice, a slave, has no legal recourse. Both Eunice, bought and brought from New Orleans, and her daughter To-mey, born into chattel slavery as her master's property, child, and concubine, are objects only of the laws of property, not of morality or family. Eunice's death has no meaning in the legal sense beyond the loss of property (though from today's vantage point it may be read variously as an act of resistance or rebel-lion).[22]

Fonsiba, Tomey's Turl's daughter, is the object of a search, a hunt for the inheritor of property, the flesh of property be-queathed a monetary boon, and the object of marriage. In both instances, Fonsiba functions in dialogic relationship to the laws and legal codes initiated by men. Her own words, "I'm free" (268), insist both on her freedom from previous constructions and on Ike McCaslin's acknowledgment of her autonomous con-dition, but they are not enough to redefine her relationally under the legal discourse that rationalizes patriarchy.

Molly Beauchamp, a free woman married to Tomey's Turl's son Lucas, has no legal standing beyond the protection of the white man she has nursed. She is doubly treated as property – by the white McCaslins for whom she is both wet nurse and unspoken but implicit gratifier of "other" needs (*droit du sei-gneur*); a vessel, an object, Molly belongs as property also to her legal husband Lucas Beauchamp whose hearth has a fire signi-fying conjugal/marital love, but whose treatment of Molly re-duces her to inanimation and boundedness within an "impervi-ous" tranquillity.

The ultimate act of ownership, however, is bodily control, especially of women. For women who are so controlled by their masters, to reproduce is not just to duplicate themselves as prop-erty, but to reproduce the image of the owner. "Reproduction," master-slave intercourse leading to reproduction, is a narcissistic act in addition to being a declaration of legal authority of not merely patriarchy (the law of the father), but also of the law of the land. "The power of the master must be absolute to render the submission of the slave perfect."[23] Incest thus guarantees the exclusive right to property. Basically in the father-daughter incest that Ike McCaslin deduces in "The Bear" (254–259), old Carothers McCaslin possesses the body of his daughter Tomasina. Her body is thus marked incest victim and is re-marked a second time as the property of the father. His sexual conquest is an act of staving off competition for property already owned and marked as owned but in the game of competitive acquisition nonetheless always vulnerable to become the object of property. In marking Tomasina's body as exclusive property, Carothers violates not legal codes regarding the right to hold property and to protect property from seizure by trespassers or transgressors, but the religious, moral, ethical, cultural, and societal codes of individual and communal conduct or behavior. That Carothers' "violation" ends in Tomasina's death (as well as in the death by self-drowning – suicide – of her mother Eunice) is not ultimately the point; the point is rather that Carothers' violation success- fully staves off all competitors for his "property" Tomasina and produces yet more property (Tomey's Turl) that is in its "white" maleness even more the image of the owner Carothers than Tomasina could ever be in her femaleness. Here is a confounding point: miscegenation that is also incestuous is a move toward the legal destruction of blacks as racially marked.

What Ike McCaslin "reads" into the plantation commissary ledger is the homosocial; the text of the ledger, multiply inscribed by Carothers, and both of his twin sons Buck and Buddy, may be deciphered as the ultimate heterosexual homosocial act – father-daughter incest, the right of the father over life, the power to create/give life and to take it away. Ike's rejection of his inherited right (by virtue of his white, male, son position) to land (and the legal and commercial traditions of the plantation) is also a rejection of his right to the masculinity and the heterosexual prerogatives figured in Carothers' sexual domination of his daughter.

Within *Go Down, Moses*, Ike's choice of the society of men, Sam Fathers, and the hunters is not necessarily a displacement of male heterosexual erotic desire, but it can be read as homoerotic attraction to the "other" of Tomasina, or Eunice; that is to say, it is an attraction to the other as reconfigured by a Sam Fathers and, ultimately, by the men of the big woods. Foucault theorizes:

It is through sex – in fact, an imaginary point determined by the deployment of sexuality – that each individual has to pass in order to have access to his own intelligibility (seeing that it is both the hidden aspect and the generative principle of meaning), to the whole of his body (since it is a real and threatened part of it, while symbolically constituting the whole), to his identity (since it joins the force of a drive to the singularity of a history).[24]

That Ike textualizes the "sin" as sexual inscribes into the ledgers his own sexual awakening and his "fear" of a biological danger implicit in any recognition of self as a sexual being. Although Foucault concludes that "Sex is worth dying for. It is in this (strictly historical) sense that sex is indeed imbued with a death instinct," he also says that in the West, bestowing a high value on love made death acceptable (Foucault 156).

When, in "Delta Autumn," the young woman descendant of Tomey's Turl asks whether Ike has lived so long that he has forgotten how to love (346), her words may be read in relation to the higher value placed on love (with the attendant suggestion of the transcending spiritual) as a way of ameliorating the necessary sexual (bodily and material) component of the intercourse that produced yet another biracial Edmonds-McCaslin-Beauchamp child. She exerts on the scene a configuration of Ike's own absent and long vacated desire for either love or sex; each has been replaced by a desire for death, but – unlike Rider in "Pantaloon in Black" – without a specific mechanism or mode of transport to death, and thus also with an all-compelling motive for death. If, configured in the ledgers, is a movement toward death (read multiple deaths – Eunice, Tomasina, eventually Carothers) in the aftermath of sex and specifically sex across racial lines, then Ike is attracted to death but repulsed by the sexual component he identifies with it. Sexuality is power and threatful as in the sexual aggression and power plays of old Carothers, who, born in 1772, is at least sixty years old when he impregnates his own daughter; Ike's own reluctant father Buck, son of old Carothers, also fathers Ike when he is over sixty.

In deciphering a homosocial message in the ledgers, Ike locates a double assault against property, ownership, and the laws protecting both. He may see his own connection to Tomey's Turl in being both motherless and fatherless, but he capitulates to the "will" of old Carothers when he attempts to disperse to Tomey's Turl's children their monetary legacies. To circumvent the authority of Carothers' legal will, to break its binding contract, would be a transgession of the expected order and the rationale behind that order. To vacate a will is to disrupt patriarchy in the site of patrimony and property. When Ike relinquishes his own claim to a paternal inheritance, he does not deny the authority of Carothers' will and its assertion of right over his black progeny. The questions of property and the dispersal of property, and proprietary rights linked to paternal rights, that Ike raises, are, from the outset of the narrative, embedded in the attention to blacks and to racial difference. Sexual crime, as Ike interprets it from the ledgers, is also linked through blacks to both property and death. It is a short step from a recognition of the problematics of slave ownership to that of land ownership; the explicit connection is the condition of the materiality. (The conquest of land is here similar to the contest of wills and black antiwill, in that the conquest is "man" against "nature," old Carothers against the wilderness in the making of a plantation and against the black as a subject in maintaining slavery.) In "Delta Autumn," the young woman as a visibly white descendant of Tomey's Turl may be located outside a discourse on the object of property. If the nature of power is reconsidered in terms of the complexity of property/law/games, then power shifts to the unnamed woman with the child. In repelling Ike's move to objectify her, she solidifies her control over her own positionality. Freedom of identity for her is possible. Subjectivity and race can be self – rather than culturally – constructed.

The Game of Compensation

Tomey's Turl's story ends in two different narratives: one in that of the young woman in "Delta Autumn" and one in that of Butch Beauchamp in "Go Down, Moses." Bracketed by textual instability, both are his relational descendants and the objects of property, and both transgress cultural codes and subvert social mandates. The one continues the rejection of property in favor of

148

the immaterial emotional, psychological connections that create society and "law," the other goes in quest of all the materiality denied to him and his ancestors and of all the external recognition of his value and worth denied him in a segregated, paternalistic society. His flashy clothing is a marker of his individual and racial visibility, and of his reclaiming his body and expressive culture as his own. These two narrative histories suspend speculation and reinscribe textual instability. The nameless woman disappears, the multiply named Butch dies. Perhaps Butch dies because he is a cipher and in an historical sense a signifier of a black man's fate between the wars. Entrapped and limited in living on the McCaslin-Edmonds place and working on shares as his ancestors had, Butch rebels against modern bondage and commits crimes against the existing paternalistic and racist order. In stealing from the commissary, he strikes out against the embodiment of economic power and exploitative control in the plantation system. But Faulkner can only envision him as the bad seed of a bad father, who must be punished for leaving the South and transgressing its political economy.

Perhaps the woman disappears because, as Lee Jenkins suggests, she is constructed out of a white fantasy, a dream of wish fulfillment and forgiveness.[25] Perhaps she disappears because she is also a reconfiguration of Tomey's Turl and because, with her infant son, she is a sign of both Tomey and Turl, who must confront the father and name his guilt and his sin (his rape and his lack of love or recognition). Described as having "moist young flesh where the strong old blood ran after its long lost journey back home" (362), the woman duplicates the reproduction of a racialized and rejected progeny. If Lucas Beauchamp could believe: "Old Carothers, he thought I needed him and he come and spoke for me" (58), then perhaps it is possible to believe that Tomey's Turl's female descendant comes back to speak for him, to talk back with the strength and passion that were silenced in Tomey and unvoiced in Turl. That both the woman and Butch are relational residents in a common text but do not come together as closure of that text returns me to a recognition of Tomey's Turl's hybridity.

Go Down, Moses may be read in terms of hybridity as an autobiographical act distanced and protected by games (masculine), forms of entertainment ("nigger stories"), distraction, and relief (hunts, cards, dice playing, gold digging). The ideological constraints of games and the textual constructions of race (and gender) function as a mask for the construction of a writerly self, autonomous and authoritative. During the period from the late 1930s to the early 1940s Faulkner was at a point of sheer frustration with his position as a writer, his lack of recognition and income, and with his position within the family, his multiple dependents, mainly female relatives but also blacks. Thus, although the narrative may appear to be an intervention against racial aggression – a dual attempt at accommodation (Ike, McCaslin, Roth) and resistance (Ike, Sam Fathers, Lucas, Rider) – and against female devaluation (Molly, Mannie, and Miss Worsham), it may also function as retribution, challenging the material support of family and the morality of family structure, even while assuming responsibility for their existence and continuance (Ike, Gavin Stevens). Social Darwinist thought in the 1890s figures as another layer of law, natural law at odds with the general right to property, but similarly disallowing a space for women and blacks under law. The "fittest" and the "survivors" may be applicable to black and white women in the final section of the narrative, "Go Down, Moses," but as terms they are also invested with meaning by the presence and actions of Gavin Stevens and the white men who act out of cultural rituals and ideologies that they cannot as "men" vacate.

Karl Zender concludes that "Faulkner helped to create the difficulties he faced by his willingness to take on responsibilities within his family and by his eagerness *to acquire property.*"[26] In his reading of Faulkner's financial burdens and "impoverishment at the time of writing *Go Down, Moses,*" Zender points to Faulkner's psychological need for property as a means of "actualizing a deeply cherished vision of his proper role in the world": "a paterfamilias, the owner of a mansion, the master of a plantation" (Zender 69). This need for property, to become the titled owner of land, Greenfield Farm, and the manor house, Rowan Oak, as well as the patriarchal master of the family, configured specifically as dependent women and black servants, is an expression of Faulkner's self-definition and self-actualization, of his game and role playing. Michael Grimwood calls this an extended period of exhaustion.[27] I call it a game of ego building through fantasies of power, racially and militaristically based, manifested in narratives of games, sport, and play.

Faulkner's own personal history, then, complicates an interrogation of property in *Go Down, Moses,* because that history suggests his reduction of human society to market relations and his elevation of political society as the protective strategy for property and the orderly exchange of property. In this view, however, those who are "proprietors" dominate both society and law. In Faulkner's case, this placed him in a position of dominion over both his white family – particularly the women as dependents – and his black servants – as the paternalistic funeral sermon for his "mammy," Caroline Barr, and his dedication of *Go Down, Moses* to her suggest.

Was Faulkner finally using "race" as a game of self-identification and self-aggrandizement? Was he playfully inscribing himself into the text of *Go Down, Moses* as "nigger," the wished-for irresponsible manipulative presence? Or as a Tomey's Turl, a hybrid construction produced within a restrictive environment yet able to invent a game within which freedom obtains? Faulkner's self-consciousness as a white, male Southerner entrapped within an unsatisfying and costly domesticity and his expressed desire for attention and acclaim as an author during the period in which he produced *Go Down, Moses* have been documented.[28] How much of *Go Down, Moses* is a self-reflexive move on Faulkner's part may be difficult to gauge, but the possibility of its being his game of arbitrary (self)compensation in which a Tomey's Turl is both the object of the wager and the subject of the deal opens up and closes out my own reflections on the text and its complexities.

NOTES

1 Change and instability seem readily observable constants in *Go Down, Moses.* If, as Norbert Elias argues in *The Civilizing Process* (Oxford: Basil Blackwell, 1978), change is the normal condition of

social life, then the representation of society in Faulkner's text adheres to the process of change as normality.

2 William Faulkner, *Go Down, Moses* (1942; rpt. New York: Vintage International Books, 1990), 257; subsequent references appear parenthetically. The information about Tomey's Turl's birth is revealed in the McCaslin commissary ledgers in "The Bear," Part 4.

3 Referred to as both "old Carothers" and "L. Q. C.," the founder of the Mississippi McCaslins takes his name from Lucius Quintus Cincinnatus Lamar, a lawyer who began his career in Oxford, Mississippi, and became a justice of the United States Supreme Court. This naming may be read as a connection between the discourses of ownership/property and law in the text.

4 A. Leon Higginbotham, Jr., *In the Matter of Color: Race and the American Legal Process: The Colonial Period* (New York: Oxford University Press, 1978), 391.

5 Patricia J. Williams, *The Alchemy of Race and Rights: Diary of a Law Professor* (Cambridge: Harvard University Press, 1991), 233. Williams takes the title, "On Being the Object of Power," from Orlando Patterson who contends that slaves cannot be the subjects of property, only the objects of property. See Patterson's *Slavery and Social Death* (Cambridge: Harvard University Press, 1982).

6 Martin J. Osborne and Ariel Rubinstein, *A Course in Game Theory* (Cambridge: MIT Press, 1994), 2.

7 Philip E. Lewis, "La Rochefoucauld: The Rationality of Play," in *Game, Play, Literature,* ed. Jacques Ehrmann (Boston: Beacon Press, 1968), 138.

8 Martha Albertson Fineman, "Introduction," *At the Boundaries of Law: Feminism and Legal Theory,* ed. Martha Albertson Fineman and Nancy Sweet Thomadsen (New York: Routledge, 1991), xiv.

9 Mark V. Tushnet, *The American Law of Slavery, 1810–1860: Considerations of Humanity and Interest* (Princeton: Princeton University Press, 1981), 157–159. See also David Brion Davis, *The Problem of Slavery in Western Culture* (Ithaca: Cornell University Press, 1966), 10, 165–166.

10 Johan Huizinga, *Homo Ludens: A Study of the Play Element in Culture* (New York: J. J. Harper Editions, Harper & Row, 1970), 32.

11 Daniel Hoffman, *Faulkner's Country Matters: Folklore and Fable in Yoknapatawpha* (Baton Rouge: Louisiana State University Press, 1989), 115.

12 Eric Dunning and Chris Rojek, "Introduction: Sociological Approaches to the Study of Sport and Leisure," in *Sport and Leisure in*

the Civilizing Process: Critique and Counter-Critique, ed. Eric Dunning and Chris Rojek (Toronto: University of Toronto Press, 1991), xi.

13 Used to explain such phenomena as cooperation, revenge, pressure, or threats, the theory of repeated games also "examine[s] the logic of long-term interaction. It captures the idea that a player will take into account the effect of his current behavior on the other players' future behavior" (Osborne and Rubinstein, *A Course in Game Theory,* 133).

14 I first noticed Faulkner's deployment of games in *Light in August;* in that text, he specifically uses the language of moves and players in a game of chess in the narration of Joe Christmas's death. During the same period of composing the stories that would comprise *Go Down, Moses,* Faulkner completed detective stories that became *Knight's Gambit* (1948), stories that also incorporate the strategies of chess.

15 Elliott Hearst and Michael Wierzbicki review the psychological literature on chess in "Battle Royal: Psychology and the Chessplayer," in *Sports, Games and Play: Social and Psychological Viewpoints* (Hillsdale, NJ: Lawrence Erlbaum Associates, 1979), 30–32, 55.

16 Huizinga, *Homo Ludens,* 66. Huizinga posits that in "its earliest phases culture had the play-character. In the twin union of play and culture, play is primary. It is an objectively recognizable, a concretely definable thing, whereas culture is only the term which our historical judgment attaches to a particular instance" (66).

17 Told by Ike McCaslin as he remembered hearing it from his cousin McCaslin (Cass) Edmonds, "Was" is a comic prefiguration of the denied obsessions of the narrator Ike and, as Nancy B. Sederberg outlines, of the more serious hunts presented throughout the narrative. She bases her reading on Henri Bergson's *Laughter: An Essay in the Meaning of the Comic* (1913); see Sederberg, " 'A Momentary Anesthesia of the Heart': A Study of the Comic Elements in Faulkner's *Go Down, Moses,*" in *Faulkner and Humor: Faulkner and Yoknapatawpha, 1984,* ed. Doreen Fowler and Ann J. Abadie (Jackson: University Press of Mississippi, 1986), 79–96.

18 William Faulkner, interview with Jean Stein, in *Lion in the Garden,* ed. James B. Meriwether and Michael Millgate (New York: Viking, 1968), 255.

19 *Allen v. Freeland,* 24 Va (3 Rand) 170 (1825). Tushnet observes that this case set out the position held long afterward that, with family slaves excepted, slaves were not unique (160–161).

20 Joseph C. Mihalich, *Sports and Athletics: Philosophy in Action* (Totowa, NJ: Littlefield, Adams & Co., 1982) 80.

21 Jeremy Bentham, *Principles of the Civil Code* (1802), in William Tait, *The Works of Jeremy Bentham,* vol. 2 (1982), 297. In addition, David Sugarman points out that "The identification of property and production relations with law is especially intense . . . given that ordinary English language uses *legal* terms to describe property . . . and that no ready-made alternative to this usage exists." "Law, Economy and the State in England, 1750–1914: Some Major Issues," in *Legality, Ideology and the State,* ed. David Sugarman (London: Academic Press, 1983), 223.

22 For example, Leon F. Litwack reasons that "Every slave had the capacity for outrage and resistance. And no slaveholding family, especially one which thought it commanded the affection and loyalty of its blacks, could know for certain when any one of them might choose to give expression to his or her outrage and what form that expression would take." " 'Blues Falling Down like Hail': The Ordeal of Black Freedom," in *New Perspectives on Race and Slavery in America: Essays in Honor of Kenneth M. Stampp,* ed. Robert H. Abzug and Stephen E. Maizlish (Lexington: University of Kentucky Press, 1986), 110.

23 *State v. Mann,* 13 N.C. 266 (1829).

24 Michel Foucault, *The History of Sexuality,* vol. 1: *An Introduction* (New York: Vintage Books, 1990), 156.

25 Lee Jenkins, *Faulkner and Black-White Relations: A Psychoanalytic Approach* (New York: Columbia University Press, 1981), 242.

26 Karl F. Zender, *The Crossing of the Ways: William Faulkner, the South, and the Modern World* (New Brunswick: Rutgers University Press, 1989), 69; emphasis added. Zender follows Joseph Blotner in pointing to the decrease in Faulkner's creative drive in the early 1940s as the cause of his creating familial and financial obligations that would disrupt his attention to writing; that would "simultaneously fill the void caused by his failure to write and be used as an excuse for it" (73).

27 Michael Grimwood, *Heart In Conflict: Faulkner's Struggles with Vocation* (Athens: University of Georgia Press, 1987), 224, 298.

28 See most recently, Thadious M. Davis, "Reading Faulkner's Compson Appendix: Writing History from the Margins," in *Faulkner and Ideology,* ed. Donald Kartiganer and Ann Abadie (Jackson: University Press of Mississippi, 1995), 238–252.

Notes on Contributors

Thadious M. Davis is Gertrude Conaway Vanderbilt Professor of English at Vanderbilt University, having also taught at Brown University and the University of North Carolina at Chapel Hill. She is the author of *Faulkner's "Negro": Art and the Southern Context* (1983) and the acclaimed biography *Nella Larsen, Novelist of the Harlem Renaissance: A Woman's Life Unveiled* (1993). Davis is also a poet.

Minrose Gwin, Professor of English at the University of New Mexico, is the distinguished author of *Black and White Women of the Old South: The Peculiar Sisterhood in American Literature* (1985) and *The Feminine and Faulkner: Reading (Beyond) Sexual Difference* (1990). She is also the editor of two nineteenth-century autobiographies – Cornelia McDonald's *A Woman's Civil War* and W. L. Clayton's *Olden Times Revisited*.

John T. Matthews, Professor of English at Boston University, is the author of *The Play of Faulkner's Language*, a seminal contribution to the study of this author, and *'The Sound and the Fury': Faulkner and the Lost Cause* (1991). He was coeditor of *The Faulkner Journal* from 1985 to 1994. His essay is a portion of his current book project on modernism and modernization in the American South, for which he holds an NEH Fellowship for 1995–96.

Judith L. Sensibar, Associate Professor of English at Arizona State University, is the author of the groundbreaking *The Origins of Faulkner's Art* (1984) and the recipient of fellowships from the NEH, ACLS, and the Virginia Foundation for the Humanities and

Public Policy toward the completion of her critical biography of Faulkner. Her work also includes *Faulkner's Poetry: A Bibliographical Guide to Texts and Criticism* (1988) and an edition of Faulkner's *Vision in Spring* (1984).

Linda Wagner-Martin is Hanes Professor of English and Comparative Literature at the University of North Carolina, Chapel Hill. Her recent work includes *Telling Women's Lives: The New Biography* and *"Favored Strangers": Gertrude Stein and Her Family*. She is coeditor of *The Oxford Companion to Women's Writing in the U.S.* and its anthology, *The Oxford Book of Women's Writing*.

Judith Bryant Wittenberg, Dean of the College and Professor of English at Simmons College, is the author of *Faulkner: The Transfiguration of Biography* (1979). She has also written extensively on Thomas Hardy, Sarah Orne Jewett, and Ellen Glasgow, and served as president of the Faulkner Society for seven years.

Selected Bibliography

Blotner, Joseph. *Faulkner, A Biography* (one volume). New York: Random House, 1984.

Brooks, Cleanth. *William Faulkner: The Yoknapatawpha Country.* New Haven, CT: Yale University Press, 1963.

Creighton, Joanne. *William Faulkner's Craft of Revision.* Detroit, MI: Wayne State University Press, 1977.

Davis, Thadious M. "Crying in the Wilderness: Legal, Racial, and Moral Codes in *Go Down, Moses,*" in Kinney, *Critical Essays,* 137–154.

———. *Faulkner's "Negro": Art and the Southern Context.* Baton Rouge: Louisiana State University Press, 1983.

Devlin, Albert J. "History, Sexuality, and the Wilderness in the McCaslin Family Chronicle," in Kinney, *Critical Essays,* 189–198.

Donaldson, Susan V. "Contending Narratives: *Go Down, Moses* and the Short Story Cycle," in Harrington and Abadie, *Faulkner and the Short Story,* 128–148.

Early, James. *The Making of Go Down, Moses.* Dallas, TX: Southern Methodist University Press, 1972.

Forrest, Leon. "Faulkner/Reforestation," in Fowler and Abadie, *Faulkner and Popular Culture,* 207–213.

Fowler, Doreen, and Ann J. Abadie, eds. *Faulkner and Popular Culture,* Faulkner and Yoknapatawpha, 1988. Jackson: University Press of Mississippi, 1990.

———. *Faulkner and the Southern Renaissance,* Faulkner and Yoknapatawpha, 1981. Jackson: University Press of Mississippi, 1982.

Gidley, Mick. "Sam Fathers's Fathers: Indians and the Idea of Inheritance," in Kinney, *Critical Essays,* 121–131.

Grimwood, Michael. *Heart in Conflict: Faulkner's Struggles with Vocation.* Athens: University of Georgia Press, 1987.

Gwin, Minrose. *The Feminine and Faulkner: Reading (Beyond) Sexual Difference.* Knoxville: University of Tennessee Press, 1990.

Harrington, Evans, and Ann J. Abadie, eds. *Faulkner and the Short Story.* Jackson: University Press of Mississippi, 1992.

Hoffman, Daniel. *Faulkner's Country Matters: Folklore and Fable in Yoknapatawpha.* Baton Rouge: Louisiana State University Press, 1989.

Jehlen, Myra. *Class and Character in Faulkner's South.* New York: Columbia University Press, 1976.

Jenkins, Lee. *Faulkner and Black-White Relations: A Psychoanalytic Approach.* New York: Columbia University Press, 1981.

King, Richard H. "Memory and Tradition," in Fowler and Abadie, *Faulkner and the Southern Renaissance,* 138–157.

Kinney, Arthur F., ed. *Critical Essays on William Faulkner: The McCaslin Family.* Boston: G. K. Hall, 1990.

Kuyk, Dirk, Jr. *Threads Cable Strong: William Faulkner's Go Down, Moses.* Lewisburg, PA: Bucknell University Press, 1983.

Lockyer, Judith. *Ordered by Words, Language and Narration in the Novels of William Faulkner.* Carbondale: Southern Illinois University Press, 1991.

Matthews, John T. *The Play of Faulkner's Language.* Ithaca: Cornell University Press, 1982.

Millgate, Michael. *The Achievement of William Faulkner.* New York: Random House, 1966.

Morris, Wesley, with Barbara Alverson Morris. *Reading Faulkner.* Madison: University of Wisconsin Press, 1989.

Muhlenfeld, Elisabeth. "The Distaff Side: The Women of *Go Down, Moses,*" in Kinney, *Critical Essays,* 198–212.

Peters, Erskine. *William Faulkner: The Yoknapatawpha World and Black Being.* Darby, PA: Norwood, 1983.

Reesman, Jeanne Campbell. *American Designs: The Late Novels of James and Faulkner.* Philadelphia: University of Pennsylvania Press, 1991.

Roberts, Diane. *Faulkner and Southern Womanhood.* Athens: University of Georgia Press, 1994.

Ross, Stephen M. "Thick-Tongued Fiction: Julia Peterkin and Some Implications of the Dialect Tradition," in Zacharasiewicz, *Faulkner,* 229–244.

Rowe, John Carlos. "The African-American Voice in Faulkner's *Go Down, Moses," Modern American Short Story Sequences, Composite Fictions and Fictive Communities,* ed. J. Gerald Kennedy. New York: Cambridge University Press, 1995, 76–97.

Rubin, Louis J., Jr. "The Dixie Special: William Faulkner and the Southern Renaissance," in Fowler and Abadie, *Faulkner and the Southern Renaissance,* 63–92.

Sundquist, Eric J. *Faulkner: The House Divided*. Baltimore: Johns Hopkins University Press, 1983.

Taylor, Nancy Dew. *Go Down, Moses, Annotations to the Novel*. New York: Garland, 1994.

Toolan, Michael J. *The Stylistics of Fiction, A Literary-Linguistic Approach*. New York: Routledge, 1990.

Utley, Francis Lee, Lynn Z. Bloom, Arthur F. Kinney, eds. *Bear, Man, & God: Seven Approaches to William Faulkner's The Bear*. New York: Random House, 1964.

Wagner, Linda Welshimer [Wagner-Martin], ed. *William Faulkner: Four Decades of Criticism*. East Lansing: Michigan State University Press, 1973.

Weinstein, Philip M. *Faulkner's Subject, A Cosmos No One Owns*. New York: Cambridge University Press, 1992.

Werner, Craig Hansen. "'Tell Old Pharaoh': The African-American Response to Faulkner," *The Southern Review*, 19 (October 1983), 711–736.

Williamson, Joel. *William Faulkner and Southern History*. New York: Oxford University Press, 1993.

Wittenberg, Judith B. *Faulkner, The Transfiguration of Biography*. Lincoln: University of Nebraska Press, 1979.

Zacharasiewicz, Waldemar, ed. *Faulkner, His Contemporaries, and His Posterity*. Tubingen, Germany: A. Francke Verlag, 1993.

Zender, Karl. *The Crossing of the Ways, William Faulkner, the South, and the Modern World*. New Brunswick, NJ: Rutgers University Press, 1989.